THE

Way

OF

Song

THE

Way

OF

Song

A Guide to Freeing the Voice
and Sounding the Spirit

SHAWNA CAROL

ST. MARTIN'S GRIFFIN ☙ NEW YORK

www.stmartins.com

Design by Sarah Maya Gubkin

Grateful acknowledgments are made for permission to use the following copyrighted material:

"The Skylark" excerpted from *Musings from a Sufi* by Kismet Dorothea Stam. Reprinted by permission of East-West Publications (UK) Ltd.

"Butterfly over the Field of Mustard Flowers" excerpted from *The Miracle of Mindfulness* by Thich Nhat Hahn. Copyright 1975, 1976, 1987 by Mobi Ho. Reprinted by permission of Beacon Press, Boston.

"Going Beyond" by Sandy Vorce. Reproduced by permission of Sandy Vorce.

"Strong and Empty" by Brenda Fingold. Reproduced by permission of Brenda Fingold.

"Circle Within a Circle" by Rick Hamouris. Reproduced by permission of Rick Hamouris.

"Midwives of Passion" by Daphne Petri. Reproduced by permission of Daphne Petri.

Music for Ganesh Mantra by Shawna Carol and Tom Cobb. Reproduced by permission of Shawna Carol and Tom Cobb.

And thank you to all who so graciously allowed their stories to be used throughout the book.

ISBN 0-312-31037-4

First Edition: June 2003

10 9 8 7 6 5 4 3 2 1

This book is dedicated to the loving memory of my mother,

who always encouraged me on my path of song.

CONTENTS

CONTENTS

ACKNOWLEDGMENTS

After nearly twenty years of practicing the Way of Song, I am grateful to the many, many people who joined me on this path. I want to especially acknowledge those who helped make this book a reality. To these dear ones I offer deepest gratitude.

To Judy Carlson for her generous assistance in reading the book and helping with editing and organizing the material.

To Susan Chiat for her invaluable assistance with all aspects of creating the book.

To Susan Osborn, who initiated me into toning during her Seeds of Singing workshop.

To my husband, Tom Cobb, for his deep love, constant support, wise counsel, and for sharing the Way of Song with me in all aspects of our life.

To Nancy Margulies for producing the Way of Song companion CD.

To Maxine Gautier, my awesome assistant, for her excellent and intelligent work.

ACKNOWLEDGMENTS

To my agent, Ned Leavitt, for making publication a reality.

To my editor, Marian Lizzi, for her encouragement, careful reading of the book, and for stewarding it at St. Martin's Press.

To Julia Cameron for her support and encouragement during the early stages of writing the book.

To Laurie Markoff for her love of the Way of Song and her tireless support of my work throughout the years.

To Patricia Buerklin for documenting all the songs sung during Spirit-Song classes.

To Shira Shaiman and Sara Koff-Levine for careful reading and advice.

To Mary Elizabeth Wheeler for walking with me in the early years.

To all who generously shared their experiences with song for inclusion in this book. In some cases, I've changed their names at their request.

And to the hundreds of women and men who have courageously participated in SpiritSong classes and workshops throughout the years.

PRELUDE: THE PATH TO THE WAY OF SONG

I stepped out onto the large stage in the ornate art deco grand ballroom of a plush downtown hotel in Boston, Massachusetts, where two thousand people were gathering for the opening plenary session of Body & Soul, a weekend conference on health and spirituality. I stood quietly for a few moments, watching the audience settling into their seats, listening to the animated musical tone of their chatter. They were unaware of my presence, the hum of lively conversation occupying their full attention. Taking a few deep breaths, I began preparing internally for the imminent moment when I would begin to sing.

I moved forward toward the center of the stage and an energetic force began pouring through me. In response I raised my arms up toward the sky as my first vocal tones began pouring out. The hum in the room instantly subsided, and the focused silence of the audience became a witness to my song. Softly at first, and then with a power that celebrated the passion and creativity of the human spirit, I sang, without words, for a full ten minutes. The feeling in the room was electric. When I finished there was a momentary stillness and then, thunderous applause.

Throughout the rest of the weekend, hundreds of people stopped to ask me about "that song." "What was that song you sang?" they asked.

"How did you do that?" Many people said they "shifted into another reality." Others asked if my song was Native American or told me, "I know that song. It's a Hawaiian song, right?"

While many people had wildly different ideas about the origins of my song, all of them agreed that it was an incredibly powerful, moving, and transforming experience. On some level the audience knew that this was no ordinary piece of music but a song somehow mysteriously imbued with the power and presence of spirit.

My history as a singer and musical composer, as well as my long-standing love of singing, led me to be standing alone onstage that day. But it was my more recent years of developing, teaching, and performing the SpiritSong technique, a process that celebrates the human connection to spirit through song, for which the conference promoters had hired me. They wanted me to open the conference by singing my own unrehearsed and spontaneous SpiritSong, created in the moment from my own direct connection to spirit.

How did I do this? Where did my song come from? And how did I come to sing in this way in front of two thousand people? The truth is that I created my SpiritSong completely in the moment. I became a vessel for the spirit of the song to move through me. Yes, I had sung it, but in reality the song had sung itself through me. While it may have seemed at first as if I was performing, my singing was not a recital in any sense. The audience was moved, not because I sang on key or have a perfectly trained operatic voice, but because they experienced an intimate and natural encounter with SpiritSong.

SpiritSong is a method for using our voices as a source of healing. It doesn't matter whether we think we can sing or not, whether we were told at an early age that we couldn't sing on key or in tune or whether we are experienced singers. There is a process that enables us to open up to our healing spirit through the vehicle of singing and let it pour through us. This process, with practice, is easily accessible to everyone. The power of voice can be used in this way for our own healing and connection to our spirituality as well as for the benefit of others.

Recall a time when you attended a performance of an accomplished musician or singer and left feeling spiritually uplifted and emotionally moved. Didn't you feel changed by the experience? We are all greatly affected when the creativity and the skill of a performer merge to capture the spark of aliveness. When this happens, it is not only because the performer is talented; it is also because he or she is present in the moment with the performance and the audience.

SpiritSong allows us to become more present, more aware of ourselves and our emotional, spiritual, and physical well-being. It is the expression of our authentic voice right now in this moment. It supports us by harnessing the spark of our creativity for our own health and happiness, releasing stress and tension as well as expressing emotions from anger to love to joy.

HOW I CAME TO THE WAY OF SONG

I am a child of the sixties. In that turbulent era I saw and heard civil rights marchers walk directly into police blockades and face brutal beatings and arrest while singing "We Shall Overcome." Singing gave them courage beyond reason. Ultimately that courage dismantled the segregated South. The racist Jim Crow laws were struck down. Seeing this happen, I became convinced of the power of song.

I grew up to Bob Dylan's theme song, "The Times They Are A-Changin'," and indeed they were. The daughters and sons of World War II veterans said, "Hell no, we won't go," to a new and unjustifiable neocolonial war in Vietnam.

I joined with more than a hundred thousand people taking to the streets in San Francisco to protest the war, fueled by music. Music was inseparable from the peace and social justice movements that defined that time. We marched to Country Joe McDonald's "Feel Like I'm Fixing to Die Rag" and Bob Dylan's "Blowing in the Wind." It was there that I learned what an awesome tool songs are in creating cultural change.

It wasn't until twenty years later that the work of Joseph Campbell became popularized and that the power of myth was broadly understood. I knew from experiencing thousands of people putting their lives on the line for peace and social justice that joining words with the emotional power of music was a potent brew in creating a new mythology. Songs were a key force in creating nothing less than a new reality.

In the eighties, while living in New York City and singing my songs in such classic venues as Folk City, I discovered another aspect of music that awed me: the power of song to heal.

In 1985, at the New York Open Center, I attended a workshop with Susan Osborn, then the lead singer with the Paul Winter Consort. She began the workshop by talking about how song is essential to our health. She compared the need to sing to the need to eat food. At that point I started crying; she looked over at me and asked the fateful question "Do you want to sing about it?"

There in a circle of fifty people I sang my soul's own song without words. In that moment I felt the power and grace of song more than at any other time in my life. Through this simple act of singing with loving witness I released my pent-up feelings and experienced a reunion with spirit.

That experience ultimately led me to found the Way of Song Center, and for nearly twenty years I have been teaching people this simple yet profound way of song. Numerous experiences initiating hundreds of men, women, youths, and elders worldwide have convinced me that we all can learn to sing our own SpiritSongs. I've had the privilege of hearing thousands of people SpiritSing and I can assure you that each person's song is unique and each song is beautiful.

SpiritSong is a powerful tool for freeing your voice, for accessing the authentic sound that is you, and for entering into spirit. It is a powerful tool for freeing the creative source itself because it is an emanation of the essential life or spiritual force. You may have already heard about the healing power of toning the free flow of sounding any combination of notes with any combination of consonants and vowels. SpiritSong builds on toning. Although it comes from our bodies, it also comes from a source that is beyond us. Our toning has a divine intelligence and that's why we call it SpiritSong.

This endless wellspring of song is ecstatic in nature. I like to say that the river of song is always flowing to the ocean of music and joy. However, if along the route our SpiritSong encounters blocks to that natural flow of joy, it will work with the blocked energy until it is released. It is because SpiritSinging will gently remove any blocks to the energy in our physical and emotional bodies that it is such a powerful tool for healing. If we practice SpiritSong on a regular basis, we can expect more freedom of expression, not only as singers but in all our activities.

Through this Way of Song, we learn a tremendous amount about our true emotions and our unique expression in the moment. This can open up a totally new understanding of the creative power within us.

HOW TO USE THIS BOOK

This book introduces you to the Way of Song through the use of simple practices that are easy to do. You will learn to harness the power of your own voice as a tool for your greater self-expression and personal healing.

Part I introduces the practice of SpiritSong, which uses the voice to sound what you are feeling in the moment. SpiritSong is the foundational practice of the Way of Song. It is the key to entering into the Way of Song, and through it you will experience directly the benefits described in this book.

Part II offers ways to expand your creative and healing relationship to song and introduces the practice of singing with others. These expanded practices are open to anyone who wants to try them. I encourage you to focus first on your daily SpiritSong practice, and then expand and experiment as you like.

The Way of Song is an eight-week program. Some of you may want to read the book through first, getting a feel for the overall technique. Then you can go back and experience the program step by step.

NOTES ON THE EIGHT-WEEK PROGRAM

Here are some important guidelines for working with the book as you follow the Way of Song program.

Proceed from chapter 1 through chapter 8, doing one chapter's practice per week.

Chapter 2 introduces the daily SpiritSong practice. Continue to do the daily practice for weeks three through eight. This is the central practice; I hope you will incorporate it into your daily routine, continuing long after the eight-week program is over.

Chapter 8 introduces a SpiritSong Circle. The Appendix offers two complete sample circle meetings for use in whole or in part, to help you begin your own circle.

Chapter 9 offers insight into other dimensions and experiences with the Way of Song.

Imagine your feet planted firmly on the ground and your arms outstretched to heaven. Now imagine a song flowing through you, freely, joyfully; sense the power that is your voice and sense the freedom that is you flowing unimpeded with your song. This is where you are going with the Way of Song. Are you ready to begin your journey?

PART I

THE

Practice

OF

SpiritSong

1

WE CAN ALL SING

"Where is your home?" asked a man of a skylark. "You build your nest on the earth, but sing your song in the sky."

"O man," said the skylark. "My home is neither the sky nor the earth. My real home is my song. Just as my wings lift me into space, so my song lifts me into the ether. It rises from my heart. And wherever it goes, I am there. I seem to you to be a little bird; but I am larger than the distances that separate my nest from where my joyful singing wells. In my song my soul takes flight, overcoming all distances and all separation, overcoming even the silence wherein my song may seem to die."

"Be thou my teacher, O skylark!" said the man.

—Kismet Dorothea Stam, *Musings from a Sufi*

THE HUMAN BODY IS AN INTRICATE AND EXTRAORDINARY CREATION designed to perfection by Mother Nature. Without even thinking about it, we are continually breathing, our hearts keep beating, our brains are constantly firing messages, and millions of cells in our bodies are being regenerated all the time. It's a good thing all this happens without any effort on our parts. We might become too busy or distracted, and forget what needs to be done!

Fortunately for us, nature has taken this into account and has designed a perfectly balanced system. But for our continued evolution and best survival, all the organs, bones, and blood in our bodies must be in good working order. When even one small part of the human system falls out of balance, it can affect the rest of our health.

THE USE OF YOUR VOICE

One important and often overlooked aspect of well-being is the unique mechanism known as the voice. The voice is built into our basic body kit for two main reasons: to release tensions and to communicate the unique expression of who we are. These two basic activities—the release of built-up physical and emotional tensions and the creative response to the complex experiences of being alive—together form a recipe for optimal health. This ideal mechanism for communication is given freely to us all. The only problem is that we often don't use it.

How we use our voices varies greatly and is affected by our upbring-ing, culture, gender, and even religious background. Many of us feel our voices were silenced as children or as adults. We yearn for the ability to communicate with ease, power, and grace. Because our voices are the main tool we use to express ourselves in our world, learning to open our vocal channel brings us the ability to be more effective, more balanced, and more alive. All of this leads to increased health and happiness. When

I began my own SpiritSong practice, using my voice to sound what I was feeling in the moment, I felt as though I had found a hidden treasure within myself—a wellspring of power and a release of feeling that often filled me with tears of gratitude.

When I meet people for the first time and tell them that I teach individuals how to reclaim their voices through the Way of Song, the most common reaction I receive is "Singing? Oh, no, I can't sing. I don't have a good voice." The belief that we can't sing is so common it is almost epidemic in our society. Unlike people in most indigenous cultures, who participate in singing and dancing, we, as a community, are starved for such creative outlets.

Many people I meet stopped singing because they had been shamed and humiliated, discouraged or silenced. Singing in our culture is usually a world of hypercriticism and perfectionism. SpiritSong opens our creative channel and allows us to absolve ourselves from these past misgivings.

We all have images of opera singers performing numerous demanding roles, each one perfectly—and in a foreign language, no less. It is a world of keen competition for a few professional positions. It is a world of glamorous stars where lowly mortals pay large sums of money to sit at the feet of the singers and adore them. It is a world where most people are judged as "not good enough." Our culture tells us that unless you are chosen, you are not talented, gifted, or disciplined enough to sing.

With the advent of recorded music, singing has been left to a few "extraordinarily gifted" professionals. Rather than exploring our own voices and our own creative expression, we pay others, in a sense, to sing our songs for us. Instead of singing with our friends and neighbors, we go to a large stadium filled with strangers and buy high-priced tickets to hear the latest supergroup express "our feelings." When we are upset or stressed out, instead of making the sounds our bodies were inherently designed to produce to release tension, we remain silent. This often leads us to go to high-priced therapists to release our stress and emotional pressure.

We endlessly consume products and services outside ourselves until we have become the ultimate addict culture, buying things or using drugs to fill a bottomless void that can never be filled with stuff. Brian Swimme, a noted mathematical cosmologist on the graduate faculty of the California Institute of Integral Studies, writes about this in his book *The Hidden Heart of the Cosmos*:

> *Consumerism is a prison whose walls and bars are the items adver-tised everywhere. We dedicate ourselves to getting those objects so that we can live encased by them. For most humans, even in the best of con-sumer circumstances, such a way of life proves unsatisfying to the core. It is simply not human finally to live a life sealed off from all conscious contact with those powers at work throughout the Earth and universe within every one of our cells. So intolerable is this sense of being out of it, of being left out, of being without any central meaning for the world, we will resort to any route to ease the pain.*

For most of history life was not like this. In cultures around the world people came together to sing, dance, and enact stories. Within these tribal gatherings there was room for individual expression. Those who needed healing received the focused attention of the community. The group members would be deeply attuned to one another as they joined their energies together through song. At these gatherings ecstatic and powerfully mystical states of consciousness would be induced. These were times of deep communion with one's self, with one's community, and with the Great Spirit.

For centuries singing has been used to bring about states of divine consciousness. In the Eastern yoga tradition, practitioners often chant twenty-four hours without stopping. In the West, Gregorian chants were sung in monasteries on a daily basis to bring the monks into a state of union with God. The deep inner peace and connection that can be achieved by chanting is being rediscovered. *Chant,* a CD recording of monks from a Spanish monastery singing Gregorian chants, went platinum. In the stress-filled world of the new millennium the deep peace instilled by sacred song has become a hit. Imagine how much more powerful it must be to *sing* these chants each day than to buy a CD and just listen.

In the Eastern spiritual traditions, from earliest recorded history, song has been understood to have profound mystical properties. Many of these traditions go back much further than recorded history; they are ancient. According to Paramahansa Yogananda, the first Indian yogi to establish teaching centers in the United States, "India has long recognized the human voice as the most perfect instrument of sound."

RECLAIMING OUR SINGING

In indigenous cultures, everyone sings, everyone dances. It is understood to be an expression of being human—something that the community shares in order to have joyous and ecstatic union with spirit and each other.

That is also the SpiritSong perspective. Everyone has a voice; everyone can sing. Each voice is unique and beautiful.

Grammy winner Paul Winter of the Paul Winter Consort says, "No one can sing *you* better than *you*. You're the

> Everyone has a voice; everyone can sing. Each voice is unique and beautiful.

expert." Therefore you can see that the only thing that needs to change is not your singing—you are already the best in the world at that—but your listening; that is to say, your understanding of your own value.

In order to change our sense of our own value, many of us have to climb over mountains of shame. A cause of the common "I can't sing" misbelief is embarrassment, which buries people's true and beautiful voices. This makes singing a painful matter, filled with shame and disappointment, for much of the population.

I have heard so many stories of students being shamed mercilessly in front of their peers by early grade school teachers. After such an experience the child, often before the age of twelve, vows never to be humiliated again and makes a lifelong decision to never sing again. Children may have been told that they have a funny-sounding voice. In this perfection-crazy culture, if your voice breaks or has any other unique qualities you are taught you should not sing. Men often suffer much more shame about singing than women because they suffered ridicule or embarrassment when their voices changed during adolescence.

Our ideas about music also stem from traditional theories of music education. For example, a music student must study classical works and music theory for many years before being considered suitably trained to compose. Traditional music educators completely discount the flow of song that arises from the wisdom of the body, regarding it as primitive and of no value. For those of you who may come from a classical music background, please do not let yourself be stopped by these pedantic judgments. If you've had no musical training, then rejoice. You don't need it to sing your beautiful SpiritSong.

I had the pleasure of teaching a joint workshop on creativity with the pianist Michael Jones. Michael, who has fourteen CDs of improvised piano music on the Narada label, shared the following story. While on break one summer from his studies at a music conservatory, he took a job playing jazz and blues piano in the bar of a local hotel. When he returned to school in the fall, he performed a piece from the traditional classical repertoire. But because he had been playing blues all summer, his fingers started playing blues notes in the classical piece. He was taken aside and told that if he wanted to play in styles outside the classical idiom he would have to leave the conservatory. Luckily for Michael he courageously decided to leave. By doing so, his very successful career as a musical improviser began.

A traditional musical education is not always so repressive. It does offer an in-depth study of one particular style of music and the technical tools needed to perform and compose in that style. For those with a passion to learn and play that music, the conservatory system is very well suited. But most of us are not that narrowly or specifically oriented. Nonetheless, our musical education from the first grade through high school is provided by teachers trained in the classical music tradition. Even if we've never set foot in a conservatory, most of us have been exposed to this style of musical education. For some of us who may have wanted to explore music as more of a personal expression, classical musical training might feel like a creative straitjacket.

In SpiritSong we can be completely free from concerns about right notes, wrong notes, good technique, bad technique. These issues, central to classical music, are irrelevant when practicing SpiritSong. Here, we are seeking to experience our most primary creative flow and to allow the deep wisdom of the body to sing. Our practice has more in common with yoga than with Western musical traditions.

The bottom line is that singing in this day and age is mostly reserved for a few famous recording artists or other professional musicians. Some of us join local church or community choirs or accompany ourselves on piano or guitar. Some try their skills at Karaoke bars or talent shows. However, we get to sing only songs by established composers. Rarely do we improvise, or feel we are allowed to express ourselves deeply through song.

SINGING WITHOUT WORDS

For most of us, our vocal self-expression is restricted to the spoken language. We express many of the things that we think and feel verbally. There is, however, a huge range of feelings and expressions that falls outside the realm of what can be expressed through the spoken language. It is unnatural to limit our self-expression only to speaking. Can you remember, as a child, squealing with delight or screaming with terror? This free use of our voice largely disappears when we become adults, with the exception of sighs of relief, the cooing of new lovers, and other tender expressions that defy words. When we use our voices only to convey language, we don't get to experience the voice's broader range. We fail to discover the tremendous joy and healing power available in the process of creative and unself-conscious sound-making.

Language is a series of symbols we use to express our feelings, ideas, and needs. It is at least one step removed from the original experience itself. Words become the mediator. This is important because the set of symbols we call language is often biased by the beliefs and thought processes of the prevailing culture, which creates, defines, and uses them. SpiritSong, on the other hand, is a direct and immediate expression of what we are feeling. Because it is usually sung without words, it doesn't rely on language to interpret our experiences and feelings.

In his book *Starseed: The Third Millennium*, Ken Carey says this about the restrictions of language:

There are those who imagine that without verbal, conceptual understanding there can be no understanding.

Understanding can be symbolized and to some extent conveyed through words, but understanding itself requires language no more than a bird requires a cage. Understanding comes only through experience. And for experience, there has never been—and never will be—a substitute.

Unless we are willing to venture into nonverbal modes of expression, our own personal and unique experience of life is going to be diluted in the water of words. This is why SpiritSong most often does not use words. SpiritSong allows direct experience and simultaneous expression of what we and we alone are feeling. This expression is not distorted by the lens of language and so it remains completely true for us.

Ken has been SpiritSinging for about two years and is also active in the Quaker community. He shares this experience of the power of sounding without words:

I was attending a Quaker meeting for worship. This is a silent meeting, unprogrammed, but people are sometimes led by the spirit to speak messages that are given to them. On this morning there had just been news that the Quaker school in Ramallah in Palestine had been badly damaged by a rocket attack. There were feelings of shock, grief, and anger in the meeting, and many stood and spoke of this.

I had the leading to stand and sing from spirit, but so many were speaking that there was no space in between to sing. Finally one elderly woman, very wise and much loved by the meeting, stood and spoke. After she sat down there was silence for a space of time. I rose and began to sing. The whole consciousness of the meeting, about two hundred people, focalized itself in my song, and the anger and grief expressed itself. The song transformed this emotion and allowed it to be released. It was an enormously powerful experience for me. I felt an immense current of energy flowing through me. I didn't fully appreciate this power while I was singing, because I was totally in the moment. But when I sat down I felt completely spent. It was not exhaustion, rather exhilaration, but there was the feeling of having gone totally to my limits and a little bit beyond. Later a number of people from the meeting spoke to me of how the song had perfectly expressed the feeling of the meeting without words and had released the negativity that had been there.

THE FIRST FOUNDATION—GROUNDING

The first process we will work with is called grounding. Grounding literally means to connect the energy system of our body with the energy system of the earth. It is an energetic hookup through the earth's gravitational pull to the ground. It is extremely useful to ground before doing intense spiritual work as well as anytime when raising a lot of spiritual energy.

One of the best books available today on ritual-making is *The Spiral Dance: A Rebirth of the Religion of the Great Goddess* by Starhawk. In it she describes the energy raised during a group process and names it "a cone of power." This is a natural state of ecstasy and spiritual connection so strong that one can actually sense a field of energy rising above the circle of people into a cone shape. Starhawk teaches that after raising this energy, participants must literally drop and touch the floor or earth, then either kneel or lie down with their heads on the earth. Contact with the earth helps ground and integrate the energy raised in a healing process.

I like to make the analogy of electricity running through a wire. When we SpiritSing, the song is like the electricity and our bodies are the conductors or wires. Just like electricity running through a wire, the energy rising from our songs needs to be grounded. If electricity runs too intensely through an ungrounded wire, the wire will burn out. This is also true of our bodies. It is important to realize that a song is a very powerful current of energy. Ungrounded singers can feel lightheaded, spacey, or "fry their circuits" if not properly grounded.

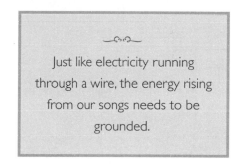

Just like electricity running through a wire, the energy rising from our songs needs to be grounded.

When I say grounded, I literally mean connecting yourself with the energy of the earth, just like the ground on an electrical wire. When SpiritSinging, grounding is done primarily through awareness; however, there are a few physical actions that help us to ground. For example, allow your awareness to go to your feet. Feel the spot where your feet meet the ground. Now allow gravity to pull your energy down even more. While standing it is important to make sure that your knees are not locked. Keep them soft and slightly bent while singing. If your knees lock up, you become cut off from the energy of the ground.

Another place where we can block energy is in the pelvic region. To loosen this often tight area of the body, gently rock the pelvis forward and back, which unblocks the energy flow.

Occasionally an individual will have a particularly difficult time grounding the energy of a song. When I first began teaching, I was working with a very large, burly man who got up to try SpiritSinging for the first time. He stood in front of me and began making deep sounds. One moment he was standing there singing and the next moment he had collapsed on top of me! The current of song had so overwhelmed him that he left his body. While this is an extreme example, that one crush of two hundred pounds taught me to make sure that everyone is well grounded before, during, and after singing.

THE SOUND FOUNDATION——BREATHING

No book on singing is complete without a word or two about breathing. After all, a song is really focused breath. In his book *Breathing: Expanding Your Power and Energy*, author and rebirther Michael Sky says, "Our greatest source of energy is breath, and our energy flow is determined mainly by the way in which we are breathing in any given moment."

It is the breath pressed upward by the diaphragmatic muscles and flowing over the vocal cords that causes our bodies to sing. If you have limited or constricted breath, you will have limited or constricted songs, and often a limited and constricted life as well. As you begin to recover your voice, you will start taking in more breath. More breath allows life energy to move more freely, which in turn allows for more feelings in our body/mind. Our songs come from these bodily feelings; therefore it is good to breathe more fully.

As we breathe more fully, deeper feelings surface, allowing us to release stress, tension, sorrow, and at times great joy. This creates more songs and ultimately more life in our life. It's a winning combination.

According to Dr. Andrew Weil, best-selling author and recognized authority on integrative medicine, "There's no single more powerful—or more simple—daily practice to further your health and well-being than breathwork." In his CD *Breathing: The Master Key to Self Healing*, Dr. Weil observes, "If today you can be aware of breathing for ten seconds more than you were yesterday, you will have taken a measurable step toward expanded consciousness, deeper communication between mind and body, and integration of your physical, mental and spiritual functions."

Have you ever watched a baby breathe? With each in-breath, the tiny belly swells and balloons outward. On the exhale the balloon lets all the air out. I've worked with many people over the years and find it astonishing how few of us breathe properly in this free and unconscious way. Many adults pull their bellies in when they take in breath. This is the opposite of the way we are organically designed to breathe.

When SpiritSinging we recommend using the "water breath"; that is, breathing in through the nose and out through the mouth. This breath slows and centers the singer. By contrast, the standard singer's breath is in and out through the mouth. In many yogic traditions this is called the "fire breath" because it helps create heat and energy. We use the water breath in SpiritSinging because it assists us with emotional connection. Rather than exciting us, it allows us to deepen our experience of self.

PRACTICES

1. Do a grounding meditation: Stand up and bend your knees. Close your eyes and feel the energy in your head. Feel it become heavy like honey, or see it as light. Then allow it to pour down into your throat, then your chest, belly, pelvis, thighs, calves, and finally into your feet. Allow it to break through your feet and pour into the ground. Feel as though your feet are anchored to the ground, as if they have deep roots attached to them. Now from the bottom of your feet sing OM.

2. Take a walk and let your feet push off the ground in every step. See if you can feel the earth pushing your feet up in each step. Let your body drop into each step, allowing gravity to pull you down. Surrender to the earth as you walk. Notice how this feels. How many steps do you take before you become distracted and forget? Do you feel more grounded?

3. Take a moment now and notice your breathing. Does your belly gently inflate when you breathe in? If it doesn't, try to relax your belly and allow it to expand while you breathe in. Otherwise, you are depriving yourself of your birthright to a natural full and deep breath.

4. At least twice every day do a "baby's breath." Place your hands over your belly, and press your hands out with your breath. Let your belly get huge as you breathe in. (If necessary, loosen any tight clothing around your waist.) As you exhale,

press your belly inward, letting all the air out completely. Wait one beat, then do another deep baby's breath in. Do at least six conscious baby's breaths. If you have a timer on your watch, you can set it to remind you to do your baby breaths. You can do these anywhere—in the car, at the office, while cooking. Breathing this way can become a habit. I hope it does!

2

THE PROCESS OF
SPIRITSINGING

The human voice is a divine vehicle that connects us with Spirit. I believe that
if we can allow Spirit to flow into us, our song can literally carry us over the
mountain.

—JOY GARDNER-GORDON, *THE HEALING VOICE*

THE PRACTICE OF SPIRITSINGING IS SIMPLY THE PROCESS OF ALLOW-
ing the healing power of song to flow through us. We start with grounding, move to the breath, and then finally are ready to begin sounding.

To begin your SpiritSong, bring your awareness to your body and to
the ground or the earth. Feel the energy in your body flowing deep into
the ground. Then imagine the earth's energy rising up through your
legs into your torso, up into your chest. Then focus on sending it back
down again. When you feel grounded, or connected with the earth, you

are ready to focus on your breathing. Use the water breath. Remember, the water breath is breathing in through your nose and out through your mouth. Breathe again. And again. Now on the next exhale allow the breath to turn into a sigh. Breathe in again and do an even longer sigh. On the following exhale let the sigh turn gently into a tone. Inhale again, and this time let the exhale become a stronger tone. Breathe and tone again. And again. And again. Listen to your sounds. To extend into SpiritSong, follow the sound, letting go of all ideas of what it is supposed to sound like. Just allow your body to lead you from tone to tone. This is how a SpiritSong is born.

Don't stop SpiritSinging until you feel a sense that the song is complete. What does complete feel like? I like to make the analogy of a wave coming into the shore. The wave naturally ends at that point when it has reached the shore and its energy is exhausted. A song's ending should feel that way—natural and gentle, complete.

Grounding, moving to the water breath, and toning are the primary vocal techniques used in SpiritSong. If you follow these simple steps, your song will flow in a very natural way. Since you are making up the "tune" as you go along, there is no need to worry about hitting the right notes.

Remember, the intention in SpiritSong is to allow your body to sing its truth, however it sounds. It may be a groan or a sweet high pitch, musical-sounding or very unmusical. The spirit of song can move through you in surprising ways. It may sound like a howl, a growl, or a shriek of joy. Or tears may come. All of this is perfect in the Way of Song.

Reaching for a particular note or tone quality is not the purpose of this Way of Song. With SpiritSong, you are free to explore the entire range of your voice. Experiment by singing sounds that are short or long, clear or strange. This is your song in the moment. This is your SpiritSong.

If you get "stuck" and think you can't SpiritSing, then go back to the beginning: ground, breathe, sigh, and tone. It may be that you feel inhibited about making sound at first. In that case start by humming; then allow the hum to open to a tone on AH.

You may also feel hesitant to begin because you can't imagine what to sing. In my experience, once you begin to tone you'll find you always have a song to sing. The flow is always available. Susan Osborn, who introduced me to SpiritSong, says, "Just reach up and grab a song." An infinite number of songs are available; all we have to do is reach out with our consciousness and our intention and, as Susan says, grab one.

After years of practicing this Way of Song I've never run out of songs to SpiritSing. The song is easy to find when you open your listening wide enough and focus carefully on each sound in the moment. This takes practice. You will find there is always another sounding to sing. Each song carries its own current or energy. The possibilities are endless.

In SpiritSinging there are no wrong notes. You just created it—how could you have created it wrong? That means there is no judging it right or wrong; we can free ourselves from the inner critic that wreaks havoc on so much of what we endeavor to do in our lives.

Laurie, a psychologist, says this about her daily practice: "SpiritSinging has helped me to find my voice and speak my truth, eased emotional and physical pain, eased my allergies, opened the flow of my writing, released some of the toxic parts of my past, helped me face my fears, and made me braver." All this from opening up to the healing power of her voice.

> In SpiritSinging there are no wrong notes.

SpiritSong can be practiced alone, with a friend or loved one, or in a sacred song circle. Each has its own healing magic and power. Singing alone is a great way to start the day, check in with yourself and your feelings, relieve workday stress, and creatively experiment. SpiritSinging with your child, partner, or friend can be a service to their health or just a lot of fun. Practicing within a circle of peers magnifies the spiritual energy and is a very powerful way to work. Part II of this book gives ideas for how you can sing in community and create your own sacred SpiritSong circle.

THE DAILY PRACTICE

But first things first. Before we share our voice with others we have to find our own voice. We need to build trust in our own ability to use SpiritSong as a healing tool for ourselves. A daily practice opens the channel to our creative and spiritual life. All you need for a daily practice is a private place to sing, a journal, and twenty to thirty undisturbed minutes.

A daily practice consists of SpiritSinging for at least five and not more than twenty minutes and then, when you have finished singing, taking ten minutes to record what you experienced in your journal.

SpiritSong practice is best done in the morning, as it literally sets the tone for the rest of the day. By doing it right away, you are telling your subconscious that you are willing to put first things first. You are honoring the pure expression of your voice before your day gets crowded with activities and responsibilities. Plus, the benefits of your SpiritSong session will last all day long.

How do you know how long to sing? Five minutes may seem incredibly short for a "serious" practice. However, musical time is very different from ordinary time. Song is so powerful you may find that five minutes is enough. On the other hand, after five minutes you may feel as if you've just gotten started.

When I work with people in a private SpiritSong session, which usually lasts one hour, some people choose to talk for fifty minutes and sing for ten. Others sing for forty-five minutes without stopping. The time you sing may vary greatly from day to day. The answer to "How long?" is "You don't know, but your body does." Set aside the time, allow your mind not to know, and then follow your body.

As you SpiritSing, you will be listening very carefully to your body and its messages. Your body is the temple of your spirit. It holds within it all your emotions and responses to life. Do you feel groggy today? Achy? Excited? Anxious? Tune in to your body and SpiritSing about it. Connect with what you feel and let the song of this moment sing through you.

When you SpiritSing, the reverberation of your song's current may cause your body to tremble or shake slightly. If the trembling becomes very pronounced it is a sign that the current is too strong and you need more grounding. If this happens, make sure you return your focus to your feet and the connection with the earth. Do this even if it means stopping the flow of your song while you reconnect with the ground.

Here are a few more suggestions for your daily SpiritSong practice. It's best to sing while standing because the lungs, ribs, and abdomen are open and spacious. If practical, take off your shoes—bare feet can help grounding. Since strong emotions may be released when you SpiritSing, you may find yourself beginning to tear up while you sing—but just keep singing. When we SpiritSing we sound right through any tears that may arise.

It is very important to ground again after you complete your song.

You can do this by mentally reconnecting your feet to the earth, or you can squat or kneel on the ground and place your hands on the floor.

After you have finished singing and are fully grounded, it is important to take a few minutes to integrate the experience. This is why it is recommended that you take ten minutes to record what you experienced in your journal. Here are several samples of journal entries by people who are doing the daily SpiritSong practice. The first two are from the journal of Sheri, a college student:

Today I set the timer for twenty minutes. Grounded for five to seven. Taking the extra couple of minutes to breathe, stretch, and feel my feet really paid off. I felt a deeper, more peaceful connection today than I have the past week or so. After grounding I toned for fifteen minutes or so. The single tones eventually turned into melodies. I had throat-clearing problems today, but not too badly. My throat ached a bit during parts of the session, so I sang about the feelings. I was able to open my eyes for the first time today and stare out the window at the snow falling as I toned.

I sang for about fifteen minutes today. Nothing came up really. Not many songs in me today. Some judgments though. I'm realizing that as soon as I achieve something, I raise my expectations. I don't want to do that. I'll try viewing my practice sessions like morning pages: just show up and sing for a while. Some days I'll sing blah, blah, blah. No judgment. Just sing. And since I am not listening, I can't determine if what came out was a good melody.

Focus instead on one thing: listen for the song. Then sing it. Some days you will hear it more clearly than others. Doesn't matter. Just show up and sing, anything, for fifteen minutes.

The next journal entries are by Patricia, a fiction writer:

My SpiritSong this morning had wild energy. With whoops and little swooping sounds and sighing, breathy sweeps downward. It was in my gut or my solar plexus—not in my head. I don't remember thinking much—just waiting for what would come next.

I heard voices coming out of me that I didn't even recognize. And there was a sense of connecting with my grandfather. I felt great strength. Intensity. Power.

You can see that each day's SpiritSinging can be very different and that journaling is a good way to reflect and integrate your experiences as well as providing a fascinating record of your journey.

Now that we know how to do the daily practice and when to do it, let's explore where to do it.

MAKING SACRED SPACE

Make sacred space
And be reminded
Of who you are.
You are spirit in body,
Sacred space.

—*GODDESS CHANT*

We practice SpiritSong in sacred space. What is sacred space? Sacred space is a protected place and time, dedicated and set apart for the purpose of connecting the self with spirit. The actual location of your sacred space is important. For your daily practice you will want to find a place where you will not be interrupted. Ideally, it will be a place where you are not concerned about disturbing others with your sound or being overheard in the intimate activity of exploring your authentic song.

If you live with other people, do what you can to make sure the other members of the household do not disturb you. Put the cat out, unplug the phone, or whatever it takes to ensure privacy. If you are concerned about interruptions, tell people, "I'm doing a practice of discovering my voice. Please don't interrupt me during the twenty to thirty minutes I need to sing in private."

After meeting the basic requirements, it is up to your creative impulses to bring as much harmony and beauty to your space as you would enjoy. Ideally, you should be able to decorate your sacred space with whatever pleases you. I sing each morning in my office in front of an altar holding a candle and objects that are sacred to me.

When thinking about what it takes to make sacred space you may feel excitement, or you may feel resistance. Resistance takes many forms. You may think, "An undisturbed thirty minutes? Impossible!" Or it might be, "A private place is out of the question. I'd have to rent another house."

This resistance offers a powerful opportunity. When you focus your intention and choose to empower the journey to reclaim your voice, something wonderful happens. The solutions to these once seemingly insoluble problems present themselves naturally and effortlessly.

One of my students who lived in a group house without a private area found a tree in a nearby park. The branches formed a covered area similar to a tepee. She would disappear inside the tree and sing freely, laughing to herself as she imagined a passerby hearing a "singing tree." Another student exercised daily in a health club with a steam room. No one else ever went in the steam room, and she loved the acoustics!

If you cannot find anyplace else, you can use your car. But I caution you not to drive and sing. That is not creating sacred space. Pull the car over to someplace peaceful and safe for your daily practice.

If you decide to give yourself the gift of song, you will find solutions to any obstacles. The real challenge is to take a stand for your voice. The details will work themselves out when you decide to take a stand.

All these instructions on how to create your daily practice are meant to guide you as you *do it*. I am reminded of a story by Barry Neal Kaufman, cofounder of the Option Institute. In telling readers how to use his book *Happiness Is a Choice*, he relates a conversation he had with a woman who told him, "I loved your book, but it doesn't work." When he asked her what she meant she said, "Well, I read it and I really enjoyed it, but I'm not any happier. So it doesn't work." Then he asked her, "Did you do it?" "Do what?" she said. And he replied, "Did you do all the things I outlined in the book to create happiness in your life?" Of course she had not.

As you practice on a daily basis, you will become attuned to your vital energy and start removing blockages to your full and free self-expression. You will begin noticing an increase in your health and vitality.

PRACTICE LEADS TO MASTERY

Why have a daily practice? Because the best way to learn to Spirit-Sing and to work with your voice is by doing it regularly, on a daily basis. In her groundbreaking and best-selling book on creativity, *The Artist's Way*, Julia Cameron shares a very powerful process for unblocking the blocked artist. She asks her readers to commit to a practice of writing what she calls "Morning Pages." Millions of people worldwide have used this technique successfully to open up to their creativity. To free up your voice and release your authentic self-expression, here we offer a similar discipline, which is to SpiritSing every morning (and to then write about it in a journal).

Priscilla, who practices SpiritSong daily, recently told me, "I sing every morning and it completely connects me to my self for the rest of the day." She told me that when she does her morning singing she allows her body to move with the sound. She went on to demonstrate, standing up and beginning to sing while moving her body in a rhythmic and flowing manner. "I feel completely alive and connected after singing in this way," she said.

> —❧❧—
>
> "I sing every morning and it completely connects me to my self for the rest of the day."

I like to define practice as "giving yourself the gift of doing what you love." Stated another way, the law of practice is: Do what you love and mastery will follow. When you love something, whether it is playing the piano, doing yoga, or playing tennis, then know that one of the greatest gifts you can give yourself is to do it daily—for fifteen minutes, for half an hour, whatever. It is much more powerful to build your mastery step-by-step, a small amount at a time on a daily basis, than to practice for three hours once a week.

Indeed, when you have begun regular practice for even a short time and skip your daily session, it will feel like missing an old friend. You will want to reconnect. When you stop or get too busy to practice, remember this simple basic Buddhist teaching and prayer: Begin again.

DO WHAT YOU LOVE AND MASTERY WILL FOLLOW

My hunger to play music started when I was very young. At age six I began playing the violin. I quit two years later in spite of thunderous threats by my disappointed father, who told me that if I stopped I would never be allowed to study music again. At the tender age of eight, I and everyone in my family understood that I had thrown away my only chance to become a professional musician.

In spite of the end of my violin career, two years later my mother bought me a guitar for my birthday, without my father's knowledge. Since I had promised my father I would forgo further music lessons as a condition for being allowed to stop my violin studies, I began to play guitar by ear. My passion for music continued without the benefit of any further formal training until I reached college and once again began music lessons.

Even though I returned to playing music after quitting the violin, deep inside I carried with me the stigma of having failed as a violinist, of having "proved" at the age of eight that I did not have the ability to make it as a musical artist.

Like you, perhaps, I swallowed the belief that only a few lucky souls have the talent, know-how, and connections to be artists. In looking at my own musical life I decided that I was not one of those chosen people, that musical success could never happen for me. Rather than delude myself into believing that I might be gifted, I almost quit music altogether.

Yet a passion inside me exceeded my nagging doubts and continued to nudge me forward. Playing guitar and singing brought me joy in my troubled teens. When I went to college I began to write my own songs, which proved to be the most compelling form of musical expression I'd ever found. Once I began to write songs, setting my poetry to music, I was thoroughly hooked, but still my youthful doubts persisted.

Throughout my college years and during the years when I had a band in New York City, I developed a daily habit of musical practice. I found I really loved playing, and the practice sessions often led to writing a new song. In 1988 I recorded my first CD, *Mystic Soul,* with Mary Elizabeth Wheeler, and received rave reviews from Grammy winner Paul Winter and other important cultural figures. *Mystic Soul* sold well locally, but nationally it was relatively unknown, and when the CD failed to sell millions, my old doubts returned with a vengeance. I went back to my old saw, "I'm not a musical genius, so why bother to practice?" Then I had a life-changing insight: Practice leads to mastery; more practice leads to more mastery.

> Practice leads to mastery; more practice leads to more mastery. Mastery is not a magical domain for a chosen few. It is available to all of us if we commit to putting in the time to practice.

Mastery is not a magical domain for a chosen few. It is available to all of us if we commit to putting in the time to practice. A great sadness lifted from deep inside me as I began to understand this. Maybe I wasn't a musical genius like Mozart or Beethoven, but over time even I could attain at least a touch of mastery.

I call this the law of practice. If we rely on this simple truth, suddenly the limits of our talents are no more. If we practice we will get better. We will be walking on the road to mastery. Never mind how much talent we have or don't have. If we practice, we *can* attain mastery.

What do I mean by mastery? Is mastery a place we get to and then stop? Is it the final destination? And how long will it take to get there? The idea of time is tricky. Most of us are impatient. We want perfection now. Throughout the years I've taught guitar, students have asked me, "How long until I can play fluidly?" There is no right answer to this question. The process of mastery is an individual progression, with each practitioner growing at her or his own rate. How much practice until mastery? Will I ever get there? These questions must be set aside and replaced with the sheer commitment, surrender to, and love of practice. We must devote ourselves to the act of practicing for its own sake, and trust that by doing this we will improve.

The road to mastery is made up of many moments—frustrating, fun, creative, boring, loving, avoiding, and much much more. We need to embrace the entire spectrum from dark to light and all the colors in between. The organic process of growth has within it ebbs and flows, dips and turns, deaths and beginnings. It is a never-ending spiral. I pass on this simple yet sage advice to you: Never give up. If you don't quit you can't lose.

It is axiomatic that if one practices, results will come in time, and yet there is a unique and strange pattern to this advancement. In his book *Mastery*, author George Leonard suggests the following pattern of development: plateau, leap, another plateau, and so on. His research shows a cycle of dramatic improvement and then a period in which, although you continue to practice, you don't seem to advance. This lull is what Leonard calls "the plateau." Then, seemingly out of nowhere, another leap forward happens, only to be followed, eventually, by another plateau.

It is very important to remember this during the plateau phase or one can easily get discouraged and quit. I often tell my beginning guitar students to "just keep putting your fingers on the strings." It is hard for them as they struggle and bumble along trying to learn their first chords. But soon, what is not working begins to work. Practice takes faith that in time mastery will follow.

THE MYTH OF DISCIPLINE

Most of us believe in a myth about the kind of discipline it takes to commit to regular practice. Discipline implies a pushing of the self, a kind of willful overdrive. Discipline conjures up a harsh, demanding taskmaster and a good soldier obeying the commander's stern orders.

This definition of discipline is not useful for the process of practice and working toward mastery. Far from obeying a slave driver, the discipline it takes to commit to a regular practice can instead be a sweet surrender. You give yourself the gift of doing what you want to do. You trust that by frequently doing what you love, you will gradually improve. So consistently practice with love. Detach yourself from having expectations about results. Then your results will be a happy daily experience along the road to mastery. This applies to practicing SpiritSong or any other talents, abilities, or creative areas that you are drawn to pursue.

I hope this new framework for discipline and practice will assist you in making the Way of Song real for yourself by doing it. Note that when practicing SpiritSong we are not practicing a performance-oriented skill; rather, we are engaged in a spiritual practice. The elements of mastery in SpiritSong are explored more in depth in the next chapter. For now the most important thing is just to get started and see what happens.

PRACTICES

1. Get up half an hour early to allow time to do your morning SpiritSinging. SpiritSing every morning for no less than five minutes and no more than twenty minutes. Make sure that you ground yourself and use the water breath when you sing. If you need a reminder about how to begin a SpiritSong, refer to the beginning of this chapter. After SpiritSinging, get out your journal and write for at least ten minutes each morning. Note anything that has come up for you during your song.

2. At the top of a piece of paper write, "I can't sing because . . ." Then complete that statement by writing down the left side of the paper ten beliefs, reasons, or negative voices that tell you you can't sing. On the right side write ten affirmations that answer the negative voices. For example, on the left side write, "My voice sounds too old." On the right side write, "My voice is beautiful just the way it is!" Pick one of the ten affirmations and sing it every morning.

3. Write a letter to the teacher, sibling, parent, or other authority figure who knowingly or unknowingly shamed and silenced you when you sang. Tell them they were wrong, and feel free to express any resentment toward them you might have held all these years. As a variation on this exercise, write a letter thanking a person who encouraged you in your singing.

3

FINDING YOUR TRUE VOICE

Be a bud sitting quietly in the hedge
Be a smile, one part of wondrous existence
Stand here. There is no need to depart.
This homeland is as beautiful as the
homeland of our childhood
Do not harm it, please, and continue to sing. . . .

—THICH NHAT HANH, "BUTTERFLY OVER THE FIELD OF GOLDEN
MUSTARD FLOWERS," *THE MIRACLE OF MINDFULNESS*

*N*OW THAT WE KNOW "HOW" TO DO IT, LET'S LOOK MORE DEEPLY into the process of SpiritSinging. Working with the practice of Spirit-Singing for many years gave me the insight that it is first and foremost a spiritual practice using singing. It is a sacred way of song. While the therapeutic benefits are many and of great value, I came to understand that these benefits are a by-product of a spiritual practice rather than an end in themselves.

While SpiritSinging may look or even sound like primal singing, it is important to understand that there is much more to the practice than the sounds that result from doing it. When we SpiritSing we are also practicing spiritual precepts that provide an ecstatic connection with self and through self to spirit. It is very important to be aware of the aspects of the practice that accompany the physical act of SpiritSinging. They are:

1. being authentically ourselves, our true selves
2. being nonjudgmental, practicing loving acceptance
3. being completely present in the moment, practicing mindfulness
4. surrendering to the current of spirit in the song—trusting spirit

AM I DOING IT RIGHT?

Even though we have been following the simple instructions in the last chapter on how to SpiritSing, the question "Am I doing it right?" might arise. This can be a natural response to doing something new. Take a moment to consider whether this feeling of uncertainty is an experience you have had in other activities of your life.

One of my SpiritSong students shared her experience of an extreme form of this self-doubt. A successful attorney, she said that before appearing in court she would become so worried about making a mistake that she would write down in her preparatory notes, "My name is

Alice Saunders. May I address the court?" for fear she might forget her own name.

Instead of feeling free and at ease within ourselves we can be plagued by an undercurrent of uncertainty and fear. SpiritSong is a deep practice of letting go of the question "Am I doing it right?" The truth is, there is no right way to do this. No sound is inherently better than another sound. The really useful question when SpiritSinging is "Am I doing it truly?"

BEING AUTHENTIC

When we are free from the concern about "doing it right," it is only natural that we will sing our own unique song. When we focus on the song within us and stop comparing it with someone else's song or with some imagined ideal song, we effortlessly sing our own true song. We find our true voice. When we sing the way we alone sing, we'll be singing the truth.

My friend Nancy shares this story of finding her true voice:

Up until a couple of years ago I was one of those people who loved music but couldn't sing. I tried from time to time when I was alone to mimic a song I heard on the radio or from a favorite record of mine. But never could I create the kind of singing I heard others sing. I had pretty much given up on that possibility when I attended a SpiritSong workshop. In that environment I discovered that if I relaxed, breathed deeply, exhaled fully, and let the sound move through me—that I could find my voice. I could sing—not for the purpose of entertaining other people or repeating a song someone else had written but much deeper than that—I could sing my own songs. There was a sound and a tone that came through me that were my personal expression of my special voice. I found that to be such a moving experience—so liberating!

Being authentically ourselves comes from letting go of judgments and being in the present. It is the ultimate freedom. Imagine simply being the way you really are, with no fear of being rejected or judged, with no demands to perform in any way other than what feels the most natural to you. This is what it means to be authentic. This is where much of the deep joy of SpiritSinging arises.

Many of us are waiting for permission to be ourselves; to have our own voices. If you've been waiting for permission, here it is: no one can be you as well as you—you have permission to be 100 percent you. No one can sing you as well as you—you have permission to sing 100 percent you.

BEING NONJUDGMENTAL

In his book *Happiness Is a Choice,* a guide for the practice of being happy even in the face of great personal challenge, Barry Neal Kaufman talks about the power of letting go of judgments. He says that dropping judgments is a major shortcut to happiness. I would add that it's also a shortcut to freeing our true voices.

When we SpiritSing we practice dropping judgments. We use the song as our focus, our point of awareness, and we practice letting go of thoughts. In this regard it is very similar to the practice of meditation and offers many of the same benefits of training one's mind to be one-pointed. I find it easier to do with song because it is a more active practice than sitting in meditation and focusing on the breath. I also enjoy the sensation and release of the sound moving through my body while at the same time getting the benefit of training my mind.

To let go of judgments we place all our attention on each sound in the moment and cease giving energy to the running commentary of the analytical mind. The analytical mind is always evaluating everything. It says, "That was a high note, that was a low note, a loud sound, a soft sound," and on and on. Then the analytical mind comments on its commentary, deciding whether what it has analyzed is good or bad.

Many times we are stopped from experiencing our true voices because we judge our songs as bad. Another way to become free of judging your voice is to decide, "It's all good." Simply observe what happens. Practice embracing what is. Your voice cracked—wonderful! It sounds funny way up high—how amazing and interesting. You start to moan when you sing—perfect! These are dramatically different attitudes than the ones we are used to, and they are freeing.

> Your voice cracked—wonderful! It sounds funny way up high—how amazing and interesting. You start to moan when you sing—perfect!

The greatest antidote I have found for all shaming singing experiences is a large dose of listening with love and acceptance. When people feel that you are not judging them, that you really want to hear them—I mean hear *them*, not perfection but where they really are and how they really sound—amazing healing can take place.

I recall a woman who sang with our SpiritSong circle for several years. When she first joined the circle she could only croak out one note, and she buried her head in shame as she sang. As shaky as that one note was, we celebrated it. Slowly, after being encouraged and accepted by the song circle many times, she began to lift up her head as more and more notes came out. It was glorious to be present for her expansion into more and more song.

OUT OF THE JAIL OF JUDGMENT

I recently worked with another woman who was a music student at a prestigious music school. Although she had auditioned and been accepted as a voice student, she hadn't sung a note since school started. When I began to work with her she had been attending the school for four years and had changed her major to composition so she would not have to sing. She reported to me that every time she tried to sing, her throat constricted and it hurt too much to sing.

After SpiritSinging and exploring her feelings, we discovered that being seen and validated by others was so important to her that the mere thought that others might not like her voice was devastating. To protect herself from being judged by others, she literally stopped herself from performing by creating a pain in her throat.

I suggested that when singing, she should imagine her internal voices of judgment and her fear of criticism as tiny little ants. I told her that if they came up while SpiritSinging, she should just brush them away as one would an ant. With practice she was able to SpiritSing and lightly brush away the negative judgments and fear that had paralyzed her. One day she walked into a SpiritSong lesson with some songs to prepare for performance. The last time I saw her she was fronting the band at a faculty recital at the music school. She turned the place on its ear!

In facilitating hundreds of people in singing, the word I say the most often is *yes*. It takes a lot of yeses to counteract the many noes we have heard in our lives. We need to practice listening to others and ourselves with a "Yes!" SpiritSong is a great big yes to you and your song.

The time to listen to yourself without any judgment is when you do your morning singing. Say yes to each and every sound that emerges. Practice developing a witness mind. That means some part of you will notice if you are judging yourself. If you are being judgmental, gently let it go and continue singing.

When we say yes to our song, the creative child within us comes out of hiding. Your child may test you, but once she is sure the mean old critic is really gone, the authentic song of your being will burst forth. The river of song always leads to the ocean of music. Our essential musician is born.

BEING PRESENT

In Buddhist Master Thich Nhat Hanh's wonderful work *The Miracle of Mindfulness*, he explains the Buddhist practice of being fully present in each moment. He describes the act of drinking tea in a mindful way:

Drink your tea slowly and reverently, as if it is the axis on which the whole earth revolves. . . . Live the actual moment. Only this actual moment is life. Don't be attached to the future. Don't worry about things

you have to do. Don't think about getting up or taking off to do any-
thing. Don't think about "departing."

Being present to our song in the moment is the practice of Spirit-Song. I recently helped a student who was having difficulty singing. She stopped in the middle of her song and said, "I feel so frustrated I can't seem to sing where I want to be." I said simply, "That's great! This is not a practice of singing where you want to be. It is a practice of singing where you *are*. Let go of your attachment to where you want to be and allow yourself to simply sound where you are now." She did, all frustration vanished, and the connection she longed for became hers. She became one with her song.

An important part of SpiritSong practice is getting "out of your mind." This sounds funny because it is also an expression for someone who is insane. We resist being "out of our minds" because there is a great fear that if we let the mind go we might become crazy, out of control. I would say that when you let the mind go, or become out of your mind, when practicing SpiritSong, you attain a state of pure relationship with song, which in turn leads to a state associated with pure meditation.

When we don't let go of our day-to-day or analytical mind, we lose the ability to hear the subtler, innate wisdom of the song. We lose the benefit of the divine wisdom that is the very nature of the song.

The way out of our minds is to allow the deep song within us to "sing us." It's sort of like a Zen koan: When is singing not-singing? When the action of singing is not an action but a reception. When we become so present to the song of the moment that we are no longer thinking or trying to make anything happen. Then we are allowing the song to sing us.

Being present means not comparing this song with any other song, either one we sang before or one that we heard another person sing. It is an absorption in each tone in each moment. It is a meditation on the song as it unfolds. It means letting go of control and allowing each note to lead to the next note. It is a yoga of song.

In his book *Yoga and the Quest for True Self*, Stephen Cope, a long-time teacher at the Kripalu Center for Yoga and Health, says:

> *When we don't try to control our energy experience, we're free to surrender to the wave of sensation, of feeling and of energy. In these remarkable moments of freedom, we can let life as it is touch us, because at our core we know that "everything is already OK." We know that the energy moving in the prana body is intelligent. We know that it is moving in just the right way for healing and full integration to happen.*

Substitute the word *song* for the word *energy* in the above passage, and read it again. This allows you to really see the parallels between yoga practice and SpiritSong practice, and it is a wonderful description of the experience of being present in your song.

SURRENDERING

I want to say just a few words on the practice of surrendering. Surrendering is much more of an Eastern concept than a Western one. In the East it is understood as a spiritual practice—to surrender the small ego to the greater spiritual flow. Satish Kumar, an Indian activist for nonviolence who walked for peace from India to Russia and on through Europe and to the United States, shares the Jain mantra of surrender in his book *Path Without Destination*:

I surrender to those who are enlightened and therefore have no enemies
I surrender to the Released Spirits
I surrender to the Wise Gurus
I surrender to the Spiritual Teachers
I surrender to the Seekers of Enlightenment

In the West, we understand surrender very differently. For most Westerners the idea of surrender is negative. It conjures up images of waving a white flag and being taken as a prisoner of war. We have been taught never to surrender, since we equate surrender with defeat. Because the word *surrender* is so negatively charged in our culture, I sometimes like to use the word *allow* instead.

Rather than surrendering to the song, we *allow* the song to sing through us. It is a receptive practice. We receive the song. This is only possible if our minds get out of the way, allowing the body to sing and let the thoughts quiet.

When SpiritSinging we seek a beginner's mind each time we sing. Why? Because the master SpiritSinger and the beginner have much in common: no expectations, a sense of fresh discovery, and a trust in not knowing. This freedom from judgment and comparing allows us to be present and authentic and also greatly enhances our ability to receive the song.

Not knowing is very powerful. In our society we have been trained to always know the answer. Yet knowing is the enemy of creativity. *Not knowing* is far more powerful in the creative act. When we don't know, there is room to discover.

> Not knowing is very powerful. In our society we have been trained to always know the answer. Yet knowing is the enemy of creativity. *Not knowing* is far more powerful in the creative act. When we don't know, there is room to discover.

A Zen story describes how a great scholar from Harvard University traveled to Japan to study with a Zen Master. When he arrived, he proceeded to expound his opinions to the Master. The Master offered him tea. When the Master poured the cup, he filled it and then kept pouring. The tea spilled out all over the table. The professor said, "Hey! What are you doing—the tea is spilling!" The Zen Master answered, "As you can see, one cannot place something in a full cup," and ended the interview.

OPENING TO ECSTASY

SpiritSong is ultimately an ecstatic practice. However, our predominately Judeo-Christian culture does not trust ecstasy. As with the fear of being "out of our minds" or crazy, we have a fear of losing control to deep pleasure. Many of us have internalized this cultural distrust of ecstasy, so that even when encouraged, we still hold back, for a fear has been instilled deep within us—a fear of our own powerful current of ecstasy.

To me ecstasy is sacred, a blessed expression of being human. It is an experience of freedom married to bliss.

If someone were to drop in on a SpiritSong circle, she or he might see people singing with their arms outstretched and their heads thrown back; people stomping their feet or pounding on a drum or singing while crying or shaking; people listening with their arms outstretched, saying, "Sing it" or simply "Yes!"

> To me ecstasy is sacred, a blessed expression of being human.

There is a truly deep pleasure in singing. A state of pure ecstasy, of pure bliss, is possible. This ecstasy encompasses both the spiritual and the physical realm, and it is the ultimate destination of our song.

My student Patricia writes about this experience in one of her journal entries.

> *I felt so empowered tonight. My song was strong. (sigh) There were voices, I don't know whose they were. There was a powerful rising energy at first. Then almost a wailing sound, and then a kind of closed in, tighter voice. It felt like an echo of someone else. It didn't feel like me. And kind of a sighing out. And my body was moving. It was like a gasping and sighing and releasing, and it was prayerful and it was ecstatic. I couldn't stop smiling when I finished. I felt great joy.*

On the way to bliss, the powerful healing energy of the song will encounter and seek to remove any blocks within the singer. It will work to remove both physical and emotional blocks, and so it may be a while—days or weeks or even months—before the new practitioner experiences this singing bliss. Be assured that the song is always moving toward the ecstasy.

PRACTICES

1. Continue your daily SpiritSinging and journaling practice as outlined in chapter 2.

2. Breathe in through your nose and out through your mouth. Next breathe in through your nose and allow the tone to come out—don't judge it or try to make it do anything—just allow it. Repeat this again and again, following the tone where it leads you. When you are done, come to silence and feel yourself.

3. Notice when you are judging yourself. If you find that you are judging and disapproving of yourself in a situation, gently ask the judge to leave and replace the unkind thought with an affirmative one. For example, if you say something in a meeting at work and notice that you thought, "That really sounded dumb," tell yourself instead, "I am well spoken." Notice what happens when you practice this.

4. Be a truth sleuth—start paying attention to when you are speaking your truth and when you are:

- Taking care of someone else's feelings
- So afraid someone else will judge you that you don't speak
- Judging yourself so harshly that you don't express who you are
- Unaware of what you're feeling.

5. Try on these new ideas this week:

- What you think of me is none of my business.
- I am the source of my own happiness.
- I cannot cause another person's unhappiness.

6. Write in your journal about how you feel about ecstasy. Do you think pleasure is dangerous, or is it sacred? Try to remember what your parents taught you about pleasure. Make a list of ten things that give you pleasure. Pick two of them and do them.

7. Give yourself a kindness date. Do something especially loving for yourself. Some examples might be to get a massage, take a long walk, or go to the movies.

8. Make a sign that says, There are no mistakes. There is only information! Post it someplace where you will see it often.

4

LISTENING IS THE WAY OF PEACE

It is the province of knowledge to speak and the privilege of wisdom to listen.

—OLIVER WENDELL HOLMES

THE PRACTICE OF SPIRITSONG IS about using your voice as an instrument of creative expression and healing. It is also about listening. There can be no healing unless our active and receptive parts are in balance. SpiritSinging is the active part; listening is the receptive.

In Western culture we place great

> There can be no healing unless our active and receptive parts are in balance. SpiritSinging is the active part; listening is the receptive.

value on the active principle—making things happen, from singing to building bridges to sending a man to the moon. The same principle creates nuclear waste and nuclear bombs.

The receptive principle is the opposite of the active mode. It is *being* versus doing. It is listening, reflecting, and contemplating. Listening fosters a relationship with others and with spirit. Most importantly, only through the receptive/listening mode can we receive spiritual guidance.

At this time, our society's active and receptive modes are seriously out of balance. Action is highly valued, but reception is not. Can you imagine being paid to meditate? When the active principle is dominant we have pollution, overpopulation, and war. When the receptive and active are in balance we have wisdom informing action, and therefore we make wise decisions about our actions. We consider not only what nuclear power can do but also what it will actually cost us, in both the short term and the long run.

Listening is the place where we receive guidance. Listening is the place where we receive our songs. When we listen to one another, listening is the place where we offer and receive loving compassion. And listening is the place where we receive the guidance of spirit.

In our culture we are taught that we receive songs from notes that an authority, "a great composer," dictates to us; we receive healing from our doctors; we receive guidance from our therapists; we receive money from our bosses; we receive connection with spirit from our minister or rabbi. The amount of disempowerment this engenders is inestimable. Receiving does *not* mean being passive, or looking to others instead of to ourselves.

LEARNING TO LISTEN

I propose that we go direct. Just as each one of us can sing, so each one of us can listen. We can receive the song our beings want us to sing, in each moment. We have music inside us that is our own. We can receive direct guidance. We can receive spirit directly. And when we choose to listen to or make music that we love, we can receive ecstatic pleasure.

Listening, like singing, is a practice. By listening I do not mean simply hearing. Listening is fully focusing our attention on what is present.

I asked Laurie Markoff, a longtime SpiritSong practictioner, to share her awareness about the listening part of her practice. She said:

I used to be distracted by my own thoughts, or too focused on the intellectual content and the effect when someone spoke to me, and now I think I can receive a wider range of input.

I think I can learn to listen deeper still, and receive more. I am interested in where this will take me. The other thing that seems to have happened is I am able to be more still and more silent. I can sit for long periods and just receive, without any noise in my head, with less interference from my own thoughts. This is a great blessing. I can even do it when I am alone, just sit and be still without thought. I could not do that before I started this practice.

LISTENING TO OURSELVES

The act of listening and the desire to be heard are closely related. All my life I wanted to be heard and I wanted to be recognized. As a child I looked to my parents to recognize me. When I became school age I looked to my teachers to recognize me, but was often disappointed. In my twenties in New York, when I was trying to get a big record deal, I thought my songs had no value unless someone else recognized them. I thought my voice had no value unless hundreds of people applauded when I sang.

Very few of us have felt deeply honored and heard by our families or our coworkers. We truly long for a deep connection with our self and with spirit, yet we believe another person must bestow the gift of this connection on us.

When we don't feel heard, we often don't listen well. We have what I call a listening deficit. We don't have the sense of ease and spaciousness that being heard creates. We don't really have the space to receive someone else. Instead, we can't wait to get what we have to say out so that we can finally be heard. When we have a listening deficit we might *seem* to be listening, but we are actually just waiting for a pause in the conversation so we can try again to be heard. In this way the listening deficit increases. There is a simple way out of this cycle: *We can listen to ourselves.*

A couple of years after I began Spirit-Singing, I was traveling in Sedona, Arizona. I was alone in my hotel, playing my guitar and singing. As I was listening to myself play I felt a great love pour over me. Then it hit me: *If you want to be heard, listen to yourself!*

> *If you want to be heard, listen to yourself!*

I didn't have to wait for a gig at Folk City in New York, or for a recording contract, or a hit song on the radio. I could give myself the gift of listening. I could bless my own song. I didn't have to wait for some outside authority to do it. Furthermore, I could have a great time with myself. I could listen while I sang and enjoy myself.

Once I realized this, my nagging sense of frustration, and the feeling that I wasn't being recognized, vanished. My ability to create increased since I wasn't waiting for some outside authority to validate me.

In the same way that I could listen to myself and appreciate what I heard, I could also listen for the still small voice of spirit. I didn't have to wait for a rabbi or a priest or a book to tell me what spirit wanted to say to me. I could wait in the silence and hear what emerged.

LISTENING TO MUSIC

One of the most delightful ways I know of practicing being receptive is to listen to music. It deepens our ability to listen and at the same time deepens our musicality. We all have access to recordings of the greatest music in the world. And here's a trade secret: Musicians don't just play music, we listen to it. We listen to lots and lots of music. We not only experience the joy of hearing brilliant and beautiful music, but we also learn and absorb what we hear. Through focused listening, musicality deepens without effort.

As a vocalist and songwriter I always listened to the vocals and the lyrics in a song. It was many years before I ever noticed the bass and drum part—they just faded into the background. All I really heard were the voice and words. When I finally heard the bass part I was amazed.

Try listening to the same piece or song several times. Each time you listen, focus on a different part or instrument. You will be amazed at how much more there is to hear.

LISTENING FOR PITCH

In music, listening has an active corollary, singing on pitch. Difficulty with singing on pitch is merely a weakness in the ability to focus and listen for the subtle differences in waveform vibrations known as frequency in physics and pitch in music.

For some people singing on pitch is a nonissue, and for some it is the root of great pain, humiliation, and the absolute certainty that they never could and never will sing. Some of you "know" that you are "tone-deaf"—an apparently incurable condition that you contracted at birth. The first thing we are going to do in exploring singing on pitch is explode the myth of "tone deafness."

Commonly a young child who has had difficulty with singing on pitch is told the lie "You are tone-deaf." Almost invariably after such a pronouncement, the child will never sing again. Real tone deafness—a physiological impairment of the hearing apparatus—is extremely rare. Difficulty with singing on pitch is much more common and almost always misnamed tone deafness, which implies hopelessness.

Just as some children naturally run faster than others, some find it easier to distinguish pitch than others. Difficulty with singing on pitch can be overcome easily with training and practice in the art of listening. All that is required is patience and practice and a large dose of non-shaming encouragement.

Let me offer a new definition of the word *patience*. I always thought that patience meant waiting. I hated to wait, so I was not too crazy about the idea of patience, which I interpreted as being happy about waiting. Then a wonderful teacher offered me another meaning. He said that patience is "being in faith." It has nothing to do with waiting; it has everything to do with being—in other words, being peaceful in the knowledge that in time the desired outcome will occur even though you don't know exactly when that is going to happen. Once again I will invoke the law of practice: *All practice leads to mastery. More practice leads to more mastery.*

There are two very different elements in recovering or uncovering our ability to hear and sing on pitch. The first involves teaching the skill set of accurately identifying different pitches. It is similar to teaching a small child to correctly identify different colors (light vibrations) as blue, yellow, or green.

The second element is working with the limiting beliefs and healing the wounding that arose out of the shaming experiences suffered about the inability to sing on pitch. These issues can cut very deep and can cause extreme difficulty in the ability to focus on the simple issue of recognizing differences in pitch.

While the actual skill can be learned quickly and easily, many times it is our beliefs about our voices that are the main block to our singing on pitch. I once worked with a man who wanted to learn to sing on pitch. He told me that he could not sing in tune. When we started working together I asked him to pick a note and sing it. I said I would join him. He began to sing a note, but after only a second he stopped, groaning and shaking his head because he felt it was not correct.

I asked him, "How could you possibly pick the wrong note when I asked you to simply make it up on the spot? I didn't establish a key. You alone are the author of the note of the moment." In my understanding, it was impossible to sing a wrong note in that situation. Yet he was so convinced that he would sing the wrong note that even in a situation where by definition it was impossible, he just kept going with that belief.

I am reminded of another story that Barry Neal Kaufman relates in *Happiness Is a Choice*. He tells the story of an emergency call from his daughter, Bryn, who suffers from an incurable heart condition called arrhythmia. This condition can be very painful for her and in fact is life threatening. On the evening described in the book, Bryn was suffering a particularly acute attack. She told him that she thought she was going to die that night.

Barry asked her if she would try to bring her heart back into a steady, healthy rhythm. This, Bryn had been told by her expert doctors, was impossible. Nevertheless, with the encouragement of her father she tried placing a stethoscope over her heart to hear the beats more clearly and began to try to control the wildly erratic beating. At first it didn't work.

Her father then asked her to carefully notice what she was listening for when she tried to control the beats. She listened carefully and found that after her heart would beat regularly for a beat or two she would *anticipate* an arrhythmic beat, which inevitably came. With that realization, Bryn focused on listening for the next rhythmic beat instead. Although she had previously believed that it was impossible, and had been told by many doctors that it was impossible, when Bryn focused on listening for healthy, rhythmic heartbeats the arrhythmia stopped. By changing her listening she changed her life.

We can listen for our next mistake or for the next time we hit a note correctly. Take time to notice—are you listening for the next wrong note? Where is your focus really—on hearing the next note that life is playing or on worrying about making yet another mistake? Our lives become filled with where we place our attention.

PRACTICES

1. Continue your daily SpiritSinging and journaling practice as outlined in chapter 2.

2. Get out your calendar and schedule a music listening session. Select CDs or artists you want to listen to for at least one uninterrupted hour. As you listen, notice how much of the music you actually hear. Do you find yourself planning your next day's meeting or reviewing the fight you had with your father-in-law? Or are you actually *hearing* the music you are listening to? Notice how many of the parts you can hear at once.

3. Better yet, check your local newspaper and go out and hear some live music.

4. Note in your journal anything that comes up for you while you practice this week.

5. Listen to and learn one new song from any of your favorite CDs.

PART II

EXPANDING YOUR SONG

SOUNDS THAT HEAL

Toning is a natural method of healing. Each time that I toned, my body felt exhilarated, alive as it had never felt before; a feeling of wholeness and extreme well-being.

—LAUREL ELIZABETH KEYES, *TONING: THE CREATIVE POWER OF VOICE*

SPIRITSONG IS A NEW WAY TO WORK WITH YOUR VOICE AND TO DIScover the healing power that resides within you. Let's face it—life is complex; everyone can benefit by learning to use their voice consciously as a healing tool for releasing ongoing stress and tension, built-up anger, depression, and sorrow. And equally, freeing the voice and expanding our ability to express love, peace, and humor can only help us in our lives.

SINGING AWAY STRESS

In today's world, stress is considered a primary cause for many debilitating diseases. We live in the most affluent part of the world and yet most people are working harder than ever and experiencing more stress as they attempt to balance busy professional and personal lives. It is a great irony that in these times, stress reduction techniques including exercise, diet, and meditation are becoming big business. Finding time to destress is fast becoming as important as breathing to our well-being.

The SpiritSong technique is a unique way to regain health and balance. It is a simple solution to the stressful blues. Sally, a purchasing manager and longtime SpiritSong practitioner, says of her experience, "It's one of the most important things I do. It gives me so much release from emotional and physical stress." You don't have to buy any special equipment, learn to operate any machinery, or join a fancy club. The main tool you need for a great stress-buster is already yours. It came with the original body kit—your voice. Why not begin now to express your life energy and creativity with greater joy, ease, and vitality?

Marlene wrote me a note after she had been SpiritSinging for only a few weeks: "The joy, the joy to sound! Since the first moment of class I've been thinking, speaking, singing in the spirit. It's as if the floodgates open, the soul sings forth its voice—I stand back and enjoy!" SpiritSong can help you to express your voice in ways that perhaps, until now, you have only dreamed about. After just one session of SpiritSinging you will see why many of my students say SpiritSong feels so good.

I regularly teach SpiritSong classes on a weekday evening. People come into class tired and dragging from a full day at work and leave feeling energized and awake. At times I begin the evening feeling exhausted, but I always finish feeling refreshed and enlivened.

I recently received a call from a SpiritSinger with whom I had not spoken in years. She is presently the codirector of an ayurvedic healing center in Colorado. She said, "I just had to call you, so often I have felt grateful for the teachings of the Way of Song. It has profoundly been a base for deep inner change, more peace and more joy."

HEALING EMOTIONS WITH THE VOICE

Besides relieving stress, SpiritSong is a healing tool for releasing difficult emotions. I have worked for some time with a woman who suffered incest as a child by her father. One of the most devastating aspects of incest is the silence that is demanded from the child who is being violated by the adult. The loss of voice, the loss of the ability to tell the truth is a serious component of this tragic abuse.

When this woman began working with me, her chest was collapsed and her voice was timid. Rather than relate the story of her incest experience, as she had countless times in therapy, she would sing without words for extended periods of time. She sometimes sang for up to forty-five minutes without stopping. With each singing session her voice got louder and stronger.

Now she holds her head up high and makes a thunderous sound when she sings. She has reclaimed a voice that was stolen from her. Each time we meet she says, with continued surprise, "I can't believe how helpful it is to me to sing this way." Not only has she been able to heal the abuse of the past, but she is also expanding her sense of self into a powerful new future.

SpiritSinging is unparalleled in helping us to release difficult emotions whatever the source. Laney Goodman, a musician who produces a national radio show called *Women in Music,* shares the following story about her experience with singing a dark pain she was carrying:

> *I took a SpiritSong workshop in Glastonbury, England, in the spring of 2002. I was there with eighteen women from the States to perform Shawna's* Goddess Chant, *a liturgy to the divine feminine. We were also traveling to sacred sites and walking in the footsteps of our ancestors on their sacred lands. The beauty of this land touched me deeply and I was experiencing deep pain and would cry a lot.*

As we were traveling to these ancient sacred places, I explored with Laney why she was feeling so much distress. She said that tuning in to Mother Earth's pain was causing her own pain. She said she couldn't stop feeling sad about how people treat the earth and each other. I suggested she could sing her pain in the SpiritSong circle we were holding later that evening.

She continues:

> *Our SpiritSong circle that night was in an ancient building on the main street of Glastonbury and we were joined by some of my fellow travelers as well as some people from Glastonbury.*
>
> *Many people in the circle sang as I sat there and experienced each of their songs . . . some of fear . . . breaking through to joy . . . some of trying to find their voice and being surprised when they did. Finally, I was moved to share my song and what I was experiencing in that moment.*
>
> *I crawled to the center of the circle because I was feeling so heavy*

with pain and emotion. I was down on my hands and knees breathing deep and crying. . . . Shawna told me to give my pain a voice . . . a sound . . . to let it out. . . . I started a low keening sound out of my belly. I began to feel and see the core of the earth and all of her fires and rocks in the center. . . . Then I saw all of the pollution and devastation in the forests and streams. . . . I saw whales beached on our shores. . . . I saw the oil slicks on the animals from oil spills. . . . I saw the crowded city streets and clouds of smog.

As I moved my sound out of my belly into my chest . . . I began to stand and feel the power of the earth moving up through my whole body, and my voice began to reflect that power. I was soon standing and moving in a slow circle . . . trancelike . . . singing through the pain that the Earth Mother and I were experiencing. Then as I moved and sang with my eyes closed, I saw an inner vision of a rainbow . . . blue skies . . . green, fertile fields. . . . Then it changed to the ocean . . . clean and sparkling. As I sang out the pain it was replaced with a sense of hope and joy.

I finally came to a stop in the center of the circle and my song took the form of a prayer . . . low and sweet. I was singing a prayer from Mother Earth, and it was one of understanding and love.

Even though I've witnessed it countless times, it never ceases to amaze me how quickly singing pain causes it to shift and ease, without any special effort. We naturally move from emotional distress to relief on the current of our true song.

I recently received a letter from a woman who attended a Way of Song workshop in Seattle several years ago.

> Even though I've witnessed it countless times, it never ceases to amaze me how quickly singing pain causes it to shift and ease, without any special effort.

When I met Koresa she was evidently very troubled. I was moved by her bravery in participating. She writes:

Dear Shawna,

I'm writing to express my gratitude for your efforts in bringing us together in a circle and creating a new beginning of sharing songs, which are transforming.

What I'm about to tell you concerns the new horizons in my life. I'm grateful and appreciative to you for being a part of my journey.

My life is filled with joy and humility these days. Now that I've discovered what have been my blocks to creative expression, I'm on a journey into the expressive arts. The spirit within me is ready to write a book and to play music.

I feel as though the coast is clear, the fog has gone away for good in some ways. In other words, nothing is standing in my way. I am now determined to write a book on behalf of children who go unheard within the foster care system in this country, from my first-hand experiences.

Little did I realize that by attending the circles of inspirational songs and singing with others, I had been planting seeds that were being nurtured to set the stage for following my real passion, which has ripened in a new way. How liberating.

I know now that life's experiences, no matter how difficult, are an opportunity. These experiences have been like a dance in the vast scope of the seeds of life, resulting in grace.

Love, Koresa

Koresa's heartfelt expression of the transforming power of song has been echoed by thousands of people who have used SpiritSong to clear old emotional wounds. When we sing, we allow the song to deeply release painful emotional energy—no matter how long we may have been holding it. Once sung, it is gone for good. It may sound simple. In fact, it is.

CHILDBIRTH WITH SONG

SpiritSinging during childbirth increases energy flow and reduces pain. Laurie Markoff, a psychotherapist and SpiritSong practitioner, relates the experience of attending her friend Gloria's labor.

It was a home birth, so it was just Gloria, her husband, and I who were present. I noticed that when she had a contraction she was breathing but not letting any sound come out. I suggested to her that she let sound out, but she seemed to find this unacceptable in some way, so I just started toning with the contractions, and then she joined me. We would tone together through the contractions, and this seemed to do a number of things—control her breath better, calm her, and allow for some release. She definitely found that this provided relief, and we used it throughout her labor, which lasted all through the night. Between the contractions we were listening to Goddess Chant, *and we would hum or sing, but during the contractions we would SpiritSing. By the time we got to the pushing stage, she was able to just allow sound to come out and help her. The whole process seemed so natural and right, as if this was the way it was meant to be done.*

In her book *Healing Yourself During Pregnancy*, vibrational healer Joy Gardner-Gordon writes about toning during labor. "As her labor progresses, a woman who is encouraged to express herself freely may make sounds similar to having a prolonged orgasm. During delivery she may scream in pain or in rapture. These sounds help to open and relax her pelvis and her cervix."

Kelly, a licensed acupuncturist, told me that she sang the entire time during labor and the delivery of her first child because it felt like the most powerful and helpful thing she could do. The breathing that she had been taught to use during delivery was nowhere near as helpful to her as toning through the contractions. The singing kept her energy up and reduced the pain.

When a delivery nurse told her to breathe instead of tone she became furious and refused. She realized that the people at the hospital didn't want to hear her—they wanted her to be quiet.

When I heard Kelly's story I decided to let women everywhere know about singing during birthing for energy flow and reduced pain. We have been silenced and kept in the dark long enough about the healing power of song and its use in our everyday lives.

HEALING THE BODY WITH SONG

While investigating the source of this powerful toning energy, Laurel Elizabeth Keyes relates in her book *Toning: The Creative Power of the Voice* how she toned for a woman who could accurately diagnose many "diseases" with a kind of X-ray vision. Here is the description Keyes shares about the experience of being witnessed by the seer:

She said that the Tone was a force she saw as swirling movement in the area of the reproductive organs, then appeared to draw magnetic cur-

rents up from the earth through the feet and limbs and rose in a spiral of light to the throat area.

When I let it pass out, freely, with no attempt to control it, it appeared to cleanse the entire body, releasing tensions and congested areas. She said that the body, afterwards, had an appearance of balance, like an engine that has been overhauled so that all parts are working together with precision, or like a harp which has been tuned and the slack strings tightened and the too-taut ones eased to make a harmonious whole.

So you can see that we can use toning and song to help with the healing of specific health or emotional problems. One of the simplest and most powerful techniques that I use for healing my body when Spirit-Singing is this: when I become aware of a pain or tension or block in a particular area of my body I bring my awareness to that part of my body and then I give it a voice. For example, if there is a tightening in the shoulder, I tune in to the tense area with my awareness and allow the sound of that place to sing. Many times a locked-in emotion is released along with the physical discomfort.

How do you know what the right sound is to heal yourself? You don't; the song does. The way to experiencing the song's knowing is to surrender to the wisdom of the song as it moves through your body and to trust the sacred song of the body as the divine intelligence that it is.

Alana is a professional photographer who was a member of my women's SpiritSong circle for many years. She shares this account of her healing journey with song:

In 1995 I was diagnosed with breast cancer. At the moment of diagnosis, my whole life flipped and I knew I must put spirit first and leave my pro-

fessional photography work. Knowing intuitively that I couldn't tolerate chemotherapy and radiation, I gathered the wisdom of many ancient and modern healing modalities. My SpiritSong practice was a central part of my medicine.

Eventually I was guided to move to Hawaii. The plants that came from Mother Earth, the ocean that washed me clean, the sweet winds that blew, and the fierce fire of Pele were my natural allies. And there was always song to tone away my fears and confusion and bring visions of hope and clear direction.

My biggest surprise and greatest pleasure came on the beach last fall, when I happened upon two friends who were talking about wanting to sing. When I mentioned my sacred song practice, they asked if I would facilitate a circle. So for the past six months, I have been teaching SpiritSong classes. It is such a gift to me to pass on my knowledge and take responsibility for myself as a teacher and healer.

THE STEPS TO HEALING WITH SONG

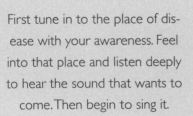

First tune in to the place of dis-ease with your awareness. Feel into that place and listen deeply to hear the sound that wants to come. Then begin to sing it.

When working with song to heal a specific block within the body, use the following process. First tune in to the place of dis-ease with your awareness. Feel into that place and listen deeply to hear the sound that wants to come. Then begin to sing it. It is important to start sounding gently at first. Resist the temptation to blast the discomfort away. Continue to follow the sound until you feel a sense of release. When giving voice to physical dis-ease, less "musical" sounds often emerge. Sounds that you might judge as outright weird are not uncommon. Let go of any judgments about how it's supposed to sound, and listen deeply to your body.

Many times you will feel immediate relief from pain and discomfort. If you do not feel a release after SpiritSinging for some time, either try a different sound or leave it for a while and return to that area of your body in your next session. Remember not to judge yourself.

After releasing the dis-ease, fill the area with a new healing tone. When you have finished sounding and releasing dis-ease, an empty space has been created where the blocked energy was. You can now tone into that space and create balance and healing, finding the healing sounds that can restore your body to health.

To do this, sound the most loving tones you can imagine into the space that has opened up. Often this can sound like a lullaby. Sound this loving song until the entire space is filled with positive healing energy.

HEALING OTHERS WITH SONG

You also can tone into someone else and assist them with restoration to health and wholeness. When doing healing work for another person, the most powerful part of the healing is your loving intention. I always say a prayer before doing any kind of body, sound, or energy healing for another person. In the prayer I offer myself as a channel for healing and ask the great love of the universe to come through me for the benefit of the person for whom I am facilitating the healing.

Fundamentally, I understand that all healing comes from spirit. It then moves through the individual healer as the vehicle for that love. Before I start a sound healing session, I always ask to open to that greater healing energy and to become an instrument of that healing. Then I can relax and allow the tones to come through me for the highest good of all concerned.

I studied a system of toning into another person with sound healer Sarah Bensen. This system requires trust of yourself and your ability to deeply tune in to what the other person needs. While I find this style of sound healing work to be quite wonderful, I am personally inclined toward always empowering individuals to deepen their self-awareness and trust their own expertise. Therefore, when toning into others, I also guide them to find their own sounds for self-healing.

TRUSTING YOUR SELF

We are an expert-oriented society. We are trained to seek expert advice before making important decisions. We are trained not to trust ourselves lest we do the most unpardonable thing: make a mistake.

It is this fear of making a mistake that takes most of us away from our voices in the first place. Brushing that fear aside is one of the most important parts of your SpiritSong practice. While you allow yourself to feel into each sound, tone, or note and let it guide you to the next one, you are actually practicing trusting yourself, your deeper self.

You are your own best expert. Nobody knows better than you do what is best for you. Some may consider this a dangerous idea. What would happen if more people trusted their inner knowing? It could cost a lot of highly paid experts a lot of money.

But what if you do make a mistake? There have been studies that show that the most successful people in life are those who make the most mistakes. They are not afraid to make mistakes, and they don't quit when they make one.

I believe there are no mistakes. There is only feedback. The feedback tells us that what we are doing is taking us either closer to what we want to create or further away. If you find you're not getting the results you desire, use life's feedback to redirect your course, getting you back on track to creating what you actually want.

SONG AND THE CHAKRAS

In practicing the Way of Song, we have been developing relationships between the body and spirit through the conduit of song. Working with the chakras is a very powerful, potent, and pleasurable way to deepen this relationship between body and spirit. Toning the chakras can bridge the material and spiritual realms.

Chakras are centers of energy located at specific points within the body. They are named after the Sanskrit word for "wheels," because each one moves in a circular pattern. Chakras cannot be perceived with the eye, yet they can be perceived through awareness. They are the translators between our physical and subtle bodies.

For centuries yogis have been aware of these energy centers and stressed their importance. According to Swami Rudrananda, an American spiritual adept in the lineage of the Indian yoga master Swami Muktananda, the chakras are "the gateways to the soul." He says, "These seven centers have a profound influence over our physiology, our mind and emotions, and ultimately our understanding."

Paramahansa Yogananda, in his book *Autobiography of a Yogi*, explains, "Awakening of the occult cerebrospinal centers (chakras, astral lotuses) is the sacred goal of the yogi. Through these divinely planned 'exits' (the seven chakras) the yogi, by scientific meditation, escapes from the bodily prison and resumes his true identity as Spirit."

Toning the chakras is a powerful practice for healing and balancing the body's energy. It is said that to have a healthy and well-functioning organism it is necessary that each chakra be balanced and unblocked. This creates not only health but the possibility of increased spiritual awareness.

Each chakra is traditionally associated with a certain location in the body and with particular qualities of mind, body, emotion, and spirit.

The first chakra is called the *root* chakra. It is located at the base of the spine right at the perineum. It is the primal center of survival and deals with the most basic issues of the body's well-being—do we need sleep or food, are we in pain? In our modern world this center can be activated by financial issues because survival now translates into the ability to keep a roof over our heads, which means having the money to pay for it. When this chakra is fully activated we feel safe in the world.

The second chakra is called the *belly* chakra. It is located in the lower abdomen, two fingers below the navel, and includes the genitals and the womb. It is our sexual center, and the focus of reproduction, sexuality, and creativity. When the second chakra is fully activated our sexuality is healthy and our creativity flows freely.

The third chakra is called the *solar plexus* chakra. It is located from the navel up to the solar plexus. It is the center of will, and the issue that centers in this chakra is whether the will is being directed by the personality or by the higher will. Another issue that can arise with this chakra is represented by the question Is there power in the will center, or has one lost the will to live? When the third chakra is fully activated our will is aligned with the will of spirit and we have powerful energy to make things happen.

The fourth chakra is the *heart* chakra. It is located at the center of the breastbone near the heart. It is the center of love—unconditional, divine love, rather than romantic love. The heart chakra is also the central chakra, integrating the three higher chakras and the three lower ones. When this chakra is fully activated we experience divine love.

The fifth chakra is the *throat* chakra. Located at the throat, it is the center of both divine and mundane communication, where our reality is communicated to the rest of the world. When the throat chakra is open and flowing we are able to communicate our truth with ease.

The sixth chakra is called the *third eye*. Located at the spot between our eyes where our eyebrows meet, it is the center of profound intuitive knowing and visionary understanding. When this center is fully activated you can perceive beyond the five senses into other dimensions.

The seventh chakra is the *crown* chakra. Located at the top of the head, it is the seat of realization, the place where we receive and transmit the most sublime spiritual energy. When activated it is represented by a thousand-petaled lotus, signifying the full bliss state sometimes known as samadhi.

When you tone into the chakras you will begin to increase your awareness of them, perceiving their distinct properties and their locations. In time you will know intuitively whether they are blocked or flowing freely.

By chanting the chakras each morning it is possible to release any blocks to the free flow of energy within them. This allows attunement and free-flowing energy throughout your emotional, spiritual, and physical body.

There are several different systems for singing the chakras. Each system is useful. In each it is absolutely critical that you *fully ground* before and after chanting.

The first system uses bija-mantras, Sanskrit seed-syllable sounds. In the yogic traditions each chakra has a specific sound, which vibrates at the chakra's frequency and stimulates its activity.

In *Music and Sound in the Healing Arts,* author John Beaulieu quotes Dr. Usharbudh Arya's (now known as Swami Veda Bharati) definition:

> *The bija-mantras are the most potent [mantras] of all. They definitely belong to no language and are not found in any dictionary. They have no gender and declensions. They are combinations of letters that represent the relationship between the kundalini (life energy) and the Supreme Consciousness.*

The bija-mantra associated with each chakra is:

> LAM—root
> VAM—belly
> RAM—solar plexus
> YAM—heart
> HAM—throat
> OM—third eye
> All sound—crown (*nada brama*, sound of the universe)

According to Kay Gardner in her outstanding book, *Sounding the Inner Landscape,* in the kundalini yoga tradition you visualize each mantra as a bright dot or flame at each chakra you utter the mantra inwardly.

I have changed this system somewhat so that rather than uttering each mantra inwardly, I sing them out loud. I suggest singing the bija-mantra of each chakra while improvising (making up) the pitch that intuitively feels right. For example, on a relatively low pitch I chant LAM, focusing on my root chakra and making sure that I feel the tone in my root chakra center. Then I move up to my belly chakra and experiment singing the bija-mantra VAM with higher tones until I find the tone that vibrates directly in my belly chakra. I move up to each higher chakra singing the bija-mantra associated with it and experimenting with higher tones until I find the tone that vibrates directly in each chakra I am singing. In this system the crown is silent, so I listen for the universal sound.

After singing all the chakras I complete the practice by singing a low tone on LAM back in the root chakra. This practice unleashes very strong energy movement and you will need to ground after you finish.

In addition to the bija-mantra or seed-syllables, there are also sounds associated with each chakra that tone and balance them.

Anodea Judith is a therapist who is an expert on working with chakras for healing. In her book *Wheels of Life,* she offers a brief description of the sounds associated with each chakra. In her system they are:

O as in Om—root
U as in Oo—belly
A as in Ah—solar plexus
E as in Ay—heart
I as in Ee—throat
MM or NN—third eye
NNG or silence—crown

Using this system to tone each chakra can be quite powerful. As described for the bija-mantras, use your intuition to decide which tones to use for each chakra.

In her book *Sound Medicine,* Leah Garfield suggests chanting each chakra out loud nine times, then waiting a minute before going on to the next. In the ancient Chinese Taoist practice there is a tradition of using multiples of three when doing sound energy work. You might want to experiment by first chanting three mantras per chakra, then six, then nine, and so on.

There is also a system that associates a specific tonal (pitch) center with each chakra. To experiment with these tones you'll need to use a piano, guitar, or even a pitch pipe to get the exact notes. I first found this system documented in Kay Gardner's book *Sounding the Inner Landscape.* I offer it to you here:

C—root
D—belly
E—solar plexus
F-sharp—heart
G—throat
A—third eye
B-flat—crown

At one time I had a residency at an artists' colony and was able to sit for many days in my studio composing. There I wrote seven pieces, one for each chakra, based on a scale built on the tonal center associated with that chakra. I find these pieces to be powerful energy medicine to balance and heal each of my chakras. I bathed myself in this music every morning for the next several years.

CHANTING THE CHAKRAS

CHAKRA	BIJA-MANTRA	SOUND	PITCH
CROWN (Spiritual awakening)	All sound (Nada brama, sound of the universe)	NNG or silence	B-flat
THIRD EYE (Intuition)	OM (Sacred syllable)	MM or NN	A
THROAT (Communication)	HAM (Ether)	I as in Ee	G
HEART (Divine love)	YAM (Wind)	E as in Ay	F-sharp
SOLAR PLEXUS (Will)	RAM (Fire)	A as in Ah	E
BELLY (Sexuality)	VAM (Water)	U as in Oo	D
ROOT (Survival)	LAM (Earth)	O as in Om	C

MEDICINE SONGS

When I was teaching at the Women of Wisdom Conference, a woman shared an inspiring story. She told us that there was a time when she was feeling so overwhelmed with sorrow she was having difficulty getting out of bed. She said that one day a song came to her about how blessed her life was, and although she didn't feel that way at the time, she began to sing it anyway. She sang the blessing song many times a day for weeks. To her amazement, she began to feel less and less sad and more and more blessed, and one day the sorrow was completely gone. This story describes a good example of what I call a medicine song.

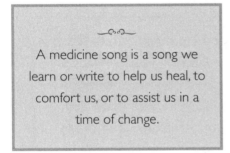

A medicine song is a song we learn or write to help us heal, to comfort us, or to assist us in a time of change.

A medicine song is a song we learn or write to help us heal, to comfort us, or to assist us in a time of change. Many times when we find a medicine song, we have an experience that the song comes from spirit and is given to us.

At one point in my life I was in a state of flux. I had moved out of my home and was camping out at a friend's studio apartment in Greenwich Village, not clear about my next move. The only thing I knew was that I had set foot on the path of sacred song and that I was prepared to follow it, although I didn't know where it would lead.

A song came to me at the time; it was really a prayer.

Oh Great Spirit, won't you find me?
I am your daughter, take me in.

I am waiting for your answer,
And I am willing to begin.

I awoke every morning for weeks with that song singing me, carrying me from dreamtime to awakening, and from uncertainty to deeper faith in spirit. I later recorded it on the *Mystic Soul* CD.

Years later, when I was serving as the core music faculty at the Omega Institute, I was having breakfast with a faculty colleague. In the course of our conversation she shared with me that she had a special chant she did each morning, a medicine chant. I asked her if she would be willing to share it with me, since I collect healing chants. We walked down a wooded path away from the noisy dining hall, then we stopped and she began to sing: "Oh Great Spirit won't you find me. . . ."

I was as startled to hear her sing me my own medicine song as she was to discover the origin of her special chant. She told me she had heard it once on a recording and it began to sing her, and that she'd been working with its medicine ever since.

SpiritSinger Brenda Fingold shared this medicine song with me recently:

Strong and empty is what I offer you.
Rooted in the earth
Reaching for the sky
Strong and empty is what I offer you.
May that I receive
May that I receive
Fill me with your light
Let me carry your word.

Brenda was at a transition time in her life. She had left a seventeen-year career as an attorney and had healed from cancer. Now she was redefining her self and her work life. She was recognizing her own strength and her willingness to serve spirit. She was empty and open to discover what was next for her. This medicine song was helping to carry her into a new life.

CHANTING AFFIRMATIONS

A particular kind of medicine song is the chanting of affirmations. The ancients were very much aware of the power of sounding intentions. The Bible says that in the beginning was the word. So powerful is the sounding out loud of intention that in the book of Genesis it is said that God spoke the entire world into being.

Affirmations work by directly giving your subconscious a new message in place of an old negative belief. It is important to state your affirmation in the present. Rather than saying, "I will have a wonderful home," say, "I now have a wonderful home." This is because the subconscious is quite literal, so our language to realign our beliefs must be very precise. When we sing, "I will have," that engenders the belief that whatever we want to create is yet to come and will forever be in the future. When we sing, "I now have," our subconscious aligns with the reality that it is here now, and soon our outer reality aligns with our new inner reality.

While it is powerful to speak affirmations out loud, it is even more powerful to sing them. When I was forty-one I was single and decided I wanted to get married. The popular press was filled with articles about the allegedly dire chances of a woman over forty finding a suitable male partner. I decided this was nonsense—that I would chant an affirmation and see what spirit would bring. I wrote the chant "I am receiving I am receiving now all the love the universe has for me." I sang it often. Soon I became involved with the man who is my husband. We were married within a year.

I recommend making short chanted affirmations to create whatever heaven on earth you want. You can also sing affirmations to counteract negative thought patterns. For example, I noticed that I was thinking, "I'm a songwriter, so I don't make any money." Once I became aware that I was thinking this thought I was amazed to discover just how frequently it came into my head. I was constantly giving myself the message that not making much money was my reality. So I set out to counteract it—I wrote a funny song to give myself a new "tape" to listen to in place of the old negative self-talk playing in my head. It goes like this:

> *I'm a songwriter. I make a lot of money,*
> *Just like the Beatles and Elton John.*
> *The songs I write are sweeter than honey.*
> *People can't help it they just sing along.*
> *I got me a carload of Grammies,*
> *I had some trouble with the IRS,*
> *Bad accountants couldn't count all my money,*
> *So I wrote another hit and got out of that mess.*
> *I got a check from ABC*
> *Bigger than the one before,*
> *And Barbra Streisand wants to record me,*
> *The press is banging at my door.*
> *Each song I write is more brilliant than the other*
> *Yet I am filled with humility.*
> *Royalties pour in internationally,*
> *I give half my millions to charity.*

I got a bonus from BMI
Reaches higher than the sky,
A TV special about me, moi, mine,
My new hit on Broadway is to die.

Be very careful how you word your affirmations. I originally wrote the above song with the line "I got me a carload of Grammies, I have troubles with the IRS." That year I got audited for the first time. As I mentioned, the subconscious is quite literal! And it brings into being what it knows.

DEVOTIONAL CHANTING

For thousands of years, people from many different cultures around the world have performed devotional or sacred chanting. They chant to connect individuals and the community with the divine.

The best-known devotional chant in the West is Gregorian chant. Gregorian chant has always captivated me. In the seventies I was a composition student at California Institute of the Arts. My first efforts in composition were to create contemporary sacred chants. When I left school I returned to my longtime passion of songwriting and had all but forgotten about my interest in sacred chant when a life-changing event happened.

In 1986 I was meditating and had a powerful vision. I saw people processing into a darkened church carrying candles and chanting, "All is growing and expanding, Blessed Be, the light has come." The church then filled with more and more candlelight and the chant became more and more beautiful with elaborate harmonies. The lyrics continued,

"And a love that's everlasting, Blessed Be, the light has come." ("Blessed Be" is a ritual blessing used by the earth-based religions that recognize Goddess as well as God.)

When the vision ended I knew that I was being asked to write a new kind of sacred music. Over the next nine years, sacred chants to the Divine Feminine came to me, culminating with the sung ritual piece *Goddess Chant*. I have been fortunate enough to be able to record these chants with some outstanding musicians. Since the release of the *Goddess Chant* CD, these new sacred chants to the Goddess continue to be sung and performed worldwide.

While Gregorian chant is still the most well-known style of devotional chanting in the West, Eastern devotional chanting is becoming more widely known. In India devotional chanting is called *kirtan* or *sankirtan*. In many Eastern traditions there is a pantheon of Gods and Goddesses rather than one God as in the Western religions. The basic principle is to chant the names of God/Goddess in praise to connect with the divine. These chants are often done in Sanskrit, a language that is imbued with sacred sound. I have spent time at a Siddha Yoga ashram where they frequently practice this style of devotional chanting. One of the chants they use at this center is *"Om Nama Shivaya,"* which means, "I bow to the divine within you." The chanting can go on for hours or even days.

Paramahansa Yogananda, founder of the Self-Realization Fellowship, speaks about these ancient Indian chanting practices. In *Autobiography of a Yogi,* he explains:

> *The Sanskrit word for "musician" is* bhagavathar, *or "he who sings the praises of God."*
>
> *The sankirtans or musical gatherings are an effective form of yoga or spiritual discipline, necessitating intense concentration, absorption in the seed thought and sound. Because man himself is an expression of*

the Creative Word, sound exercises on him a potent and immediate effect. Great religious music of East and West bestows joy on many because it causes a temporary vibratory awakening of one of his occult spinal centers [the chakras]. In those blissful moments a dim memory comes to him of his divine origin.

Here are several traditional devotional mantras, chanted in Sanskrit, for you to try.

The first one is a chant to the Hindu deity Ganesh, remover of obstacles and protector. (Another name for Ganesh is Ganapathi.) The mantra is: "*Om Gum Ganapatayei Namaha.*" It means "Om and salutations to the remover of obstacles, Ganapathi."

GANESH MANTRA

The second mantra is "*Om Namo Bagavate Vasudevaya.*" It means "Om and salutations to Vasudevaya" (Krishna's father). It is a prayer to have one's soul empowered for increased consciousness. This mantra can be chanted while circulating energy through the chakras.

OM NAMO BAGAVATE VASUDEVAYA

The third mantra, "*Om Nama Shivaya,*" means "I bow to the divine within you."

OM NAMA SHIVAYA

Traditional

Om Na- ma Shi- va- ya

Om Na- ma Shi- va- ya Shi-

va- ya Na- ma Om Shi

va- ya Na- ma Om Shi-

va- ya Na- ma Om Om na Shi-

va- ya Shi- va- ya Na- ma

Om Shi- va- ya Na- ma

Om

The mantra "*Om Mani Padme Hum*" is taken from the Buddhist tradition. It means "the jewel in the lotus." The jewel represents a clear (awakened) mind, and the lotus represents a compassionate heart. This is a central mantra in Tibetan Buddhist practice.

OM MANI PADME

The mantra "*Om Kriya Babaji Nama Om, Jai Jai Babaji Nama Om*" is a chant to the realized being Babaji, a saint from Tamil India. *Kriya* means "action with awareness," and *jai* means "victory." I was initiated into Babaji's kriya yoga in 1993 and have felt the presence of his being as a spiritual boon ever since.

OM KRIYA BABAJI NAMA OM

Music by Shawna Carol

Om kri- ya Ba- ba ji   Na- ma om

ja- i ja- i Ba- ba- ji

Na- ma   om

ja- i ja- i Ba- ba- ji

Na- ma om

In his book, *Path without a Destination,* Satish Kumar talks about a meeting with a Tibetan Buddhist nun. During their meeting she shared these insights about where to focus while chanting:

> *"The mind makes you leap either into the past or into the future—like a wild horse. The sound of the chant is used by the Self as reins to guide the mind. Meditating on the full meaning of the mantra which we chant, we can come to the realization of our true being. For example, we*

chant, Om Mani Padme Hum, *which means, I am the jewel in the lotus [slight variation in the translation]. Now, we don't need to think of the meaning of the words,* linguistically. *The real meaning is in immersing our whole being into the pure sound of the chant. When we are enchanted by the chant, we need not indulge in the intellectualization of concepts. We simply become the chants, we become the jewel, we become the lotus, we become ourselves."*

In essence she is directing us to get out of our minds when we chant. Sound familiar? She concludes: "The more you chant, the more powerful and charged that chant becomes."

You can try singing one or more of these devotional chants in the sacred space where you do your daily SpiritSong practice. Traditionally one repeats the mantra 108 times. You may have seen strings of sandalwood beads called japa beads. These have 108 beads so you can place your fingers on a bead for each repetition and know you've completed 108 when you reach the end of the beads. I find that I feel energized by singing these mantras even for only a short time. Experiment with what feels right to you.

PRACTICES

1. Continue your daily SpiritSinging and journaling practice as outlined in chapter 2.

2. Schedule a sound healing session with yourself. First scan your body for any tension, pain, or blocked energy by gently toning while slowly moving your awareness to each place in your body. After the general body scan, return to any place of discomfort and allow it to sing. Keep singing until you feel a release. Then tone love and healing energy into that place.

3. For a week, in addition to your daily SpiritSong, chant or tone the seven chakra centers. You may choose any one of the systems presented in this chapter and use it every day or experiment with trying several different methods of toning the chakras, perhaps trying different systems on different days. Make sure to ground before and after doing this.

4. Make two columns on a piece of paper. Write a list of ten negative thoughts on the left side, and next to each write an affirmation that would replace that negative thought. For example, left side: I'll never meet the right partner. Right side: I now have the perfect partner. Or I'll never be able to sing/I now sing with grace and beauty. Pick two of them and make up two little chants. Sing your affirmations every day.

5. Pick a devotional chant and learn it. Try singing it the traditional 108 times.

6. Watch for miracles. Make a note in your journal of any miracles that you noticed the day before.

SONGMAKING:
THE CREATIVE FLOW

For songwriters—indeed, for all creative artists—play is very serious business! It is the primary pathway to the most fertile field of the imagination.

—BARBARA L. JORDAN, *SONGWRITER'S PLAYGROUND*

E'VE JUST EXPLORED MEDICINE SONGS AND CHANTING AFFIRmations, both of which use words in song. We are now going to look deeper into the way words arise from the heart of song.

Since the moment you began SpiritSinging you have been composing music. You have been creating songs out of thin air. Many of us hear the words *composing music* and compare ourselves to some great composer we admire, and we don't even dare begin. But when I say *composing* I simply mean making up sounds.

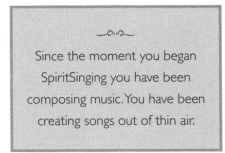

Since the moment you began SpiritSinging you have been composing music. You have been creating songs out of thin air.

The artist and writer Julia Cameron calls our internal creative artist, who finds these songs and all our other creative projects, a child. Like a small child the artist within us needs tender encouragement and many hours of experimentation and play. This chapter is designed to help you play with songwriting.

Now that I've used the word *songwriting,* notice if the thought came up for you, "Songwriting—*I can't write songs.*" If it did, stop now and create an affirmation: "I [your name] write delightful songs." Now spend a few minutes singing it.

We are all singers, and we are all songwriters. The idea that you can't write songs is just as invalid as the idea that you can't sing. Like many people, you may believe that writing songs means notating them on music paper. If you don't know how to write and read musical notation, then you think you can't possibly write songs. But musical notation is just a system for documenting the stuff you make up. With the advent of the tape recorder you can document your music even more accurately than by using traditional musical notation.

I recently met a man who worked as a professional musician. He was a superb pianist in one of the most musically sophisticated styles: jazz. When we began talking he confessed with a great deal of shame that he did not read music. Yet he composed and performed very harmonically and rhythmically complex music.

I use this example to show that musical notation is only a system for communicating to other musicians the music that you have made up. It is only one of many tools used by people who practice the craft of music.

It is by no means a measure of talent, ability, or musical creativity. If you know how to use it, great. If you don't, it does not matter one bit.

I have been a songwriter for more than twenty years. The joy, power, and release I feel when I use song to express what is in my heart and mind carry me through my life.

I have a saying: "No matter how bad things get in my life, I can always get a good song out of it." Pain can become a gift in our lives when we convert it from despair into a creative act.

When we turn painful situations into artistic expressions, we stop being victims of those situations. When a pain becomes a song, a dance, or a poem, we find that we can respond to the challenges that life presents us with in creative and positive ways. I also discovered that many times the songs I wrote to express and heal myself touched and healed other people as well. That was an amazing side benefit to giving myself the gift of songmaking.

WHAT MAKES A SONG

So let's look more closely at what makes a song. A song is words—also called lyrics—and a melody made of pitches in a specific rhythm. Just three things: words, melody, and rhythm. (The definition of a song does *not* say you have to play guitar or piano, or be in tune.) A song is a single melody with words; it is not the chords that accompany it. Anyone with a voice can create a song, whether accompanied by an instrument or not.

A question that always comes up when talking about songwriting is "Which comes first, the music or the words?" The answer is "Either." Sometimes people write the words and then set those words to music.

Other times the melody comes first and words are found to go with the music. And yet again it may happen that the words and music just seem to come out together at the same time. While exploring song-making we will experiment with each way to create a song.

SONGWORDS

The first way to create a song is by using what I call songwords. These are words that arise directly from the current of your SpiritSong. They are unlike spoken words because they arise from the sounds made by SpiritSinging. These songwords come from the part of your brain that produces music, and it brings forth a different language; the effect and experience are quite different from those of ordinary speech. For example, songwords seem to rhyme more often and to be chosen more for the way they sound than for what they mean. As in the practice of free associating, these are words that spring from a deep place within us.

To experience songwords you need to allow the current of song to be your dominant awareness, and let the words rise up out of the song. Do not think of what you want to say and then sing it—that uses your analytical mind, the part of your brain that normally produces language. You should have a firm practice of SpiritSinging without words before you try to attune to the subtle words that arise from the song. Otherwise you might become distracted by your more practiced analytical mind and sing normal speech, which is frankly boring when sung.

Here is an account of a songwords practice session from Sheri Lair's journal:

I decided to try some songwords. What a nice song came out! I did not try to make it anything. I just concentrated on what I was feeling and what words or syllables emerged. I don't remember today's song but it was called "Sweet Cinnamon Sunflower Snow Song." The word passion *emerged and I sang through it.* Gentle *emerged, too. It was a sweet song and felt good to sing. It is very liberating. I felt like I was on the edge of something, but safe. I flicked any distractions away, but there were surprisingly few. One thing is for sure: this is the most free singing (in all senses of the word) that I have ever done. And yet there is also a sense of returning in it. Now I feel happy and relaxed. I will try this again and see where it takes me.*

I originally developed the concept of songwords during a SpiritSong class. One of my students, an attorney, tended to go on and on when talking (probably an asset in his profession). One evening the entire class started going to sleep as his story droned on and on so finally I interrupted and asked if he would be willing to sing us his story instead of talking it. At first he resisted, but then he agreed to try it, and suddenly we were all laughing and crying at his tale. The singing brought out a deep well of creativity and play in this serious lawyer—and my awareness of songwords was born.

I was sharing this insight with Deena Metzger, the author of a popular book on writing, *Writing for Your Life,* and she expressed an interest in knowing more about songwords. So I went alone into the hills behind her Topanga Canyon home and sang about it into a tape recorder. This is what I sang that day:

This is the way of the songword. You reach deep.
You surrender; surrender your need to do it "right."

Allow us to sing you. Allow us to sound you, the words we have found you.
This is the way we teach you, reach you.
Oh, travel—the words travel on the song.
The words travel on the song, on the current they move.
Like electricity through a wire, water, earth, air, and fire—feel it shake
your soul. Open to the words that go along—on the current of a song.

Directly after singing this I wrote in my journal:

First you have to work with learning the current of song. This must be done without words. That is why we must practice SpiritSong first without words. SpiritSinging is a long-term practice and should be returned to always. It is the current of the song and one's intimacy with it, one's fluidity with the current itself, the raw current of song, that enables the words to flow upon it. It is essential to have a current that flows unimpeded to flow the words upon so that they move freely and fluidly. Just as one needs an unbroken wire to flow electricity.

Take a moment and think of a topic that is on your mind. For example: my mother's house. Then begin to SpiritSing. Bring your full attention to the sound. After you have made a strong connection with the song, see if any words bubble up from the sound about your topic.

STARTING WITH WORDS

Another way to create a song is to start with writing the words, or lyrics. Lyrics most often are rhymed and metered, and the sounds of the words are almost as important as the meaning of the words in a song. To bring out the magic in the sound of words, a repeated pattern of rhyme is often used. Here's an example from a song of mine:

> *What a price I have paid*
> *For the lessons I learned*
> *What it cost me in pain*
> *For the bridges I burned*
> *I keep trying to forget*
> *But the memories return*
> *What a price I have paid*
> *For the lessons I learned*

Notice that the rhyme scheme or pattern is a rhyme at the end of every other phrase. As with most lyrics, you can see that there is a repeating rhythmic pattern, or meter, to the words. Read them out loud and you will hear the repeating rhythm.

Here is another example, from my musical, *Only Business Matters*:

> *It's a one martini, two martini, three martini lunch*
> *Or mix a batch of Bloody Marys and call it brunch*
> *We all left the office as sober as a judge*
> *But when we get back from lunch—our minds are full of sludge*

This song has a different rhyme scheme called a rhymed couplet, a good rhyming device for comedy writing. The ends of every two lines rhyme with each other.

STARTING WITH MUSIC

Music, no matter how complex, is made up of small phrases. The *Harvard Dictionary of Music* says that a musical phrase is "somewhat comparable to a clause or a sentence in prose." Experiment with singing until you find a short phrase you like. Repeat it many times until you can remember it, or sing it into a tape recorder. Then make up a second phrase that feels as if it answers the first phrase. When you have found two or more phrases that you enjoy, listen to them deeply and sense what words might express the feeling of the music. Then add words to the musical phrases. Experiment with several different sets of words to the same musical phrases and see what feels best. This is how songs that begin with music are created.

SONG FORMS

There are different forms for the lyrical and musical organization of a song. A simple folk song or chant usually repeats just one musical section. For example, Bob Dylan's "Blowing in the Wind" is all one musical phrase repeated over and over—sometimes we hear new lyrics and sometimes he repeats the same lyric. If we give a letter to each musical idea, this is an AAAAA song form. The section of repeated lyrics is called the refrain. The familiar song "Happy Birthday to You" is also an AA song.

When there is a very strong chorus, or "hook" as it is called, then it is a verse and chorus form, or ABAB. An example is the Beatles' "I Want to Hold Your Hand" or Cyndi Lauper's "Time After Time."

Sometimes pop music uses a third musical idea or section, called a bridge, that is often very different musically from the first two sections. When we analyze the song form, we label the bridge section C. The bridge generally appears only once in a song, to give our ears a rest from the repeated musical material we've already heard.

If you become seriously interested in writing songs there are several wonderful books on form and technique. A good book on the subject is *Song-writer's Playground* by Barbara L. Jordan. For writing lyrics I recommend Sheila Davis's, *The Craft of Lyric Writing*. Although it is an excellent text, I don't recommend reading it until you have been writing for at least a few months.

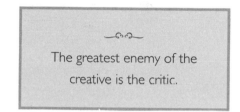

The greatest enemy of the creative is the critic.

While it is full of good information, it may stimulate your inner critic in a way that can be discouraging for absolute beginners.

Practicing nonjudgment is the most important thing to remember when songwriting. The greatest enemy of the creative is the critic. Make a deal with yourself to remain free of judgment. Remember that the song-maker in you is a small child; treat your child to large doses of encouragement. Don't kill your baby songwriter by comparing yourself to the great geniuses of the ages. Just enjoy the journey.

If you find you are judging yourself, stop and write down the judgment. Then write an affirmation to answer the judgment. Sing it every morning as part of your singing session. Many people find they are surprised and delighted by the small songs and chants they create this way. Above all, have fun!

PRACTICES

1. Continue your daily SpiritSinging and journaling practice as outlined in chapter 2.

2. Add a songwords session to your morning SpiritSinging practice. Each day sing a small songword improvisation. Try affirming what you want the day to be like. Just let it emerge. For example: "Today I am free and happy. I shall write no less than an hour of the book I want to write. And it will be good, I know—and I will have something wonderful to show—at the end of my day. It always goes this way—when I sing, when I sing."

3. Write a personal prayer and then create a song or chant using it. Include in your prayer gratitude for what you have as well as what you want to create. In Buddhist practices it is traditional to conclude each prayer by saying, "May all beings be happy. May all beings be at peace." Sing your prayer when you are doing your morning SpiritSong practice.

4. Look at the lyrics of one of your favorite songs. Read the words out loud. Notice when the lyrics rhyme; notice the rhythmic pattern in the words themselves, without the music.

5. Now listen to that same song. Notice when a musical idea is repeated. Notice when a new musical phrase comes in, and when the song returns to the first musical idea. Give each new musical

section a letter. Write down each time you hear a new or repeated section. The result might look like this: AABABCA (the form of many pop songs).

6. Write for five minutes in your journal answering the question "What is my soul's deepest desire?" After journaling, take what you have written and create lyrics from it. Notice whether you hear any music in your head as you write. Then sing the lyrics.

7. Write for five minutes in your journal about your relationship to food, including your favorite foods as well as how you feel about food in general. After journaling, take what you have written and create lyrics from it. Then sing the lyrics. See if the music you create about food is different from your writing about your soul's desire.

8. In the above two practices, I picked topics to demonstrate that you can write a song about anything. Pick another topic at random, and write about it for five minutes in your journal. After journaling, take what you have written and create lyrics from it. Then sing the lyrics.

9. Freely sing into a tape recorder. Notice any repeating phrases. Pick a phrase and repeat it; then find a musical answer to that phrase. Then listen to your song until you get a sense of what words might express the feeling in the music. Maybe you notice that it feels like summer, or that it feels like sailing, or that it feels very sad. Write words that tell that story, and notice if the syllables sing well on each note. This

is very simple, but can take years of practice to perfect—so have fun and leave the judge outside the door. After you've created your words, record yourself singing them together with the melody. A small chant or song will emerge.

10. Take a moment and bring to mind your teachers. Allow yourself to feel your gratitude toward them. Then set a timer. Give yourself seven minutes to write a song thanking one of your teachers for her or his gift to you. At the end of seven minutes, record your song.

7

SINGING WITH A PARTNER

Listening is a magnetic and strange thing, a creative force. . . . When we are listened to, it creates us, makes us unfold and expand.

—BRENDA VELAND, *IF YOU WANT TO WRITE*

UNTIL NOW YOU HAVE BEEN FOCUSING ON YOUR OWN VOICE. You've been practicing with it, loving it, and deepening your own creativity with it. It has been a relationship between your voice and you, and hopefully, a relationship between your voice and your "higher self" as well. It has been a private time of exploration and a deepening of your inner self.

Now you are going to begin exploring your voice in relationship to another person's voice. One of the greatest pleasures I've ever experienced is singing with other people. The beauty and power of voices raised together brings me an indescribable amount of joy.

Although this is a particular kind of relationship—a singing relationship—many of the issues common to all our relationships may come up. Are we kind and patient with each other? Do we listen to each other? Are we honoring of one another? Can we be authentic with someone else? Hopefully, the answer will be yes.

For your SpiritSong session together, use the same rules as for your morning SpiritSong practice. Make sure you have a protected space to sing in and that you won't be overheard or interrupted. You might want to read this chapter together before you begin.

BEING HEARD

The first way to experience singing with a partner is to take turns SpiritSinging individually. First one of you SpiritSings while the other receives the song. Then you switch, the first singer becoming the witness and the witness becoming the SpiritSinger. I suggest you sing with your eyes closed to help keep your focus on the song.

For some of us the introduction of another person who will hear us sing brings up a pressure to perform. The question "Am I doing it right?"—which we may have experienced when we began our practice—might arise again. Although these issues about performing express themselves differently for different people, I have found they all boil down to the same fear: "I will do it wrong and then be humiliated by someone seeing me do it wrong."

Gloria felt a powerful anxiety before SpiritSinging with another person present. This anxiety was so intense that she would often feel sick to her stomach. As we explored together why she was feeling so uncomfortable, she shared a memory of Christmas with her family when she was a child: the children were made to rehearse coming down the stairs and opening their presents so they would look right for their grandmother's video on Christmas morning.

As we explored the significance of this story, Gloria came to understand that the price of her "doing it right" for the video was losing her authentic voice, her authentic delight in Christmas. Gloria also realized that to reclaim her authentic voice as an adult she had to reframe her experience. She chose to focus on the awareness that SpiritSong is a practice of being with the song in each moment, not a performance. She decided that her free-flowing energy and expression were more important than her old family adage, "Do it right."

To free yourself from self-consciousness when singing with a partner, focus your attention on the sound you are making in each moment. This releases the problem of "doing it right."

THE POWER OF WITNESS

Singing together is both a great way to "play" together and a great way to practice harmonious relationship and communication. When we practice SpiritSinging with a partner, we also practice a deep and honoring listening to one another. We serve as loving witness to each other's song.

The act of being witness to someone's song is a great honor. It is a sacred trust. Empowering people to *be* themselves freely in the moment

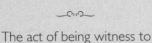

The act of being witness to someone's song is a great honor.... As we witness one another, a communion of healing and unity is created.

is a practice of a very special kind of loving. As we witness one another, a communion of healing and unity is created. Our hearts truly open to each other as we embrace each other's song as it is. Practicing with a friend or loved one can be both a wonderful way to keep up the flow of song in our lives and a very loving and intimate way to share time with each other.

I will never forget the first time I sang with another person. My dear friend Susan and I decided to try SpiritSinging together. First she sang and I received the song, and then we switched. Afterward, we sat out on the lawn and watched the sky. At the time, I felt awkward because it was the most intimate encounter I had ever had with someone other than a lover. In many ways it felt as though we had made love, even though there was nothing at all sexual about our encounter. After I got used to the intimate nature of SpiritSinging with a friend, I found it one of the most beautiful ways I have ever experienced to spend time with someone.

This may seem obvious, but be sure to pick a singing partner who likes to sing. It would be ideal for your partner to work with this book but it is not required. Look for a partner who is kind and accepting, supportive, and excited about exploring her or his own creativity. If your selected partner is new to SpiritSinging, take time to explain how it is a way of singing without words. In the event that you are also experimenting with songwords, explain and demonstrate them. Share your excitement and experience with your practice so far.

Even if your singing partner is a family member or a good friend, try to reframe the relationship for the time that you are singing together. Imagine your singing partnership as one of partners-in-creativity.

Imagine that when you are singing, you are singing for spirit, not for your partner. Imagine you are singing your soul song for a greater connection with your self, and through self to spirit. The person who is with you is not someone hearing you sing, but rather a support person, a witness, helping you to sing spirit. And you also will fulfill that role for him or her.

RECEIVING YOUR PARTNER'S SONG

When receiving your partner's song, practice listening with acceptance and a deep sense of wonder. Try to synchronize your breaths. Let go of any idea you might have about what your partner is singing about or how she or he might be feeling. Just let the sound wash over your body. Continue to send love and support to the singer. In time, you might get an impulse to take an action to support the song. It might feel right to pick up a drum and play along or to hold the singer's feet to assist in grounding.

Monitoring the singer's grounding is an important part of the listener's role. If the singer begins to go out—that is, tremble intensely, or if the eyes begin to roll back—directly intervene by holding their feet. In the extreme situation where the energy is moving very fast and the singer is actually losing balance, you should interrupt the song and bring the singer back into their body. In most cases, the singer's grounding will be firm, and no action will be needed.

The act of being a loving witness to someone as they sing is very powerful indeed. It allows that person to feel seen, recognized, and validated, because seeing is believing. There is little in life more powerful than being witnessed in our truth and being honored for who we truly are. When another witnesses you in your practice, the deep vulnerability and beauty of singing become an act of love and affirmation.

Providing loving witness also creates a circle of safety. It is very helpful to know that we are not alone when powerful emotions surface, as they often do when a song flows. As a witness, we are providing support for the singer to have a deeply personal encounter with the song. In witnessing, we say, "You are not alone, you are seen and honored, I trust you in your own process, you are worth listening to." The act of witnessing is a gift we give one another. The act of singing is a gift we give first to ourselves and then to the world.

SINGING TOGETHER IN UNISON

We begin our partnership in song by taking turns individually Spirit-Singing. After we have practiced alternately singing and witnessing with our partner, the next thing to explore is singing together at the same time.

We start by singing in unison. Unison means singing the same notes at the same time. This is the easiest and simplest way to organize two or more people sounding together. If you're both doing the same rhythm, that helps create a sense of unity.

MUSICAL DIALOGUE

The next level of singing together we call a sung dialogue. One partner sings a phrase, and the other responds. A musical dialogue ensues. This can be done with eyes closed or eyes open. The important thing is to listen very deeply to one another. Notice what sounds, phrases, tones, vowels, and rhythms your partner is singing. Experiment with sending back exactly what you heard; then try answering with a different response. This is really the essence of musical improvisation.

SPIRITSINGING AT THE SAME TIME

Finally, there is SpiritSinging together at the same time. This is a very rich way to be with each other, and it can also be challenging, especially if you don't listen carefully to each other.

Imagine trying to talk to someone while that person is talking to you. Nobody is listening, and noise, frustration, and miscommunication result. Now consider a symphony. How is it possible that so many voices can play together and make such exquisite sound? There are underlying ways of relating sounds that are musical or harmonious in nature. These ways of relating in song include echoing the phrase you have heard your partner sing, and finding a note that sounds harmonious with the note your partner is singing. And you can always join your partner in singing the same note.

It helps to establish relationship and lines of communication. One way to do this is to have one person lead for a time while the other follows. To practice leading and following, try this mirror movement exercise before you sing: Begin by facing each other. One of you will move, and the other will mirror that movement. Then switch roles. Finally, experiment with switching roles in a fluid manner, passing the leadership back and forth, communicating with eyes, body, and touch. Now you're ready to try it in song.

Consciously allow your partner to be the leader, and experiment with ways to follow your partner's song. Then switch to being the leader. As you practiced in the mirror exercise, see if you can communicate who is leading and who is following. You will experience the blending of your two different songs into a dance of harmony and dissonance or tension and release. This takes a lot of listening, communication, and trust. It also takes patience. Enjoy the process of discovery.

> You will experience the blending of your two different songs into a dance of harmony and dissonance or tension and release. This takes a lot of listening, communication, and trust.

COMPLETING YOUR SESSION

After singing, it is useful to take time to talk and process your experience together, sharing your reactions. For example, you might share whether it was more comfortable for you to lead or to follow, or whether judgments came up for you, or how sublime a particular moment felt. In addition to opening the channel of song, this can be a profound way to explore how you work in a trusting relationship.

Does the old shame that went away when you were alone come up when someone else is listening? Can you trust another person to join you in exploring your love of singing? Can you relax and have fun with this, or is it all work? Can you stay authentic, or do you try to please your partner? All the issues that can come up in a relationship can be reflected in the singing session. Use your journal to record what you learn from your experience with your singing partner.

PRACTICES

1. Continue your daily SpiritSinging and journaling practice as outlined in chapter 2.

2. Ask someone to be your singing partner. Make a specific singing date. Make sure to find a space where you will be uninterrupted.

3. With your singing partner, do the mirror movement exercise. Begin by facing each other. One of you will move and the other will be the mirror. Then switch roles. Then try switching roles in a fluid manner, passing the leadership back and forth, communicating with eyes, body, and touch.

4. With your singing partner, decide who will SpiritSing and who will receive first. Practice honoring each other by listening without judgment, with a "yes!"

5. With your singing partner, sing a song you both know in unison. If your partner is of the opposite sex, you may have to sing in different octaves, depending on your range.

6. With your singing partner, tone in unison (on the same note). Try to match tone quality and volume. Alternate starting the tone and matching it with each other.

7. Engage in a song dialogue. One person sings, and the other then answers. Play off each other. Listen deeply and have fun.

8. While singing together, experiment with rhythm. One person could use hand-clapping or a simple hand drum or shaker while the other sings to that rhythm. The singer makes up a song in the moment to go with the rhythm. Then switch roles.

9. Take a few minutes to talk about what the experience of singing together was like for each of you. Talk about your own experience; do not analyze your partner's experience. You might each want to spend a few minutes journaling about the experience of singing together. See if you would like to make another singing date—and if the answer is yes, schedule it.

8

CREATING A
SPIRITSONG CIRCLE

We are a circle
Within a circle
With no beginning
And never ending

—RICK HAMOURIS

S SPIRITSONG CIRCLE IS A JOURNEY BACK TO THE ROOTS OF song and the sacred circles of our ancestors. The increased flow of life force and creativity you have already experienced by doing your singing practice alone is powerfully amplified when you come together in a community to do this practice.

Singing together in a sacred circle, alternately being the singer and witness, is the most powerful form in which to practice SpiritSong. The circle holds a space for you where it is possible to go deeper. If you are afraid, there is a sense that you are not alone and are being supported. The circle creates an energetic container for the singer, composed of loving intention and shared practice.

I cannot emphasize enough the depth of love that is shared by a group that SpiritSings together. In the Boston area, where the Way of Song Center is located, we have spawned many song circles, musical groups, deep friendships, and even marriages. The sense of communion with the source of life that is experienced by the circle is a blessing for all concerned.

I want to acknowledge that to invite a group of friends to SpiritSing together may seem like a big stretch. Remember back to the resistance you may have experienced when you first decided to find a time and place to do the morning SpiritSong practice. While some of you may feel excitement about forming a song circle, others will experience that familiar feeling: resistance. We tell ourselves we are too busy, too tired, or too shy. We tell ourselves "Nobody will want to come and do this." We think we can't possibly find a room large or private enough for a group of people to sing undisturbed.

The list of creative expressions of resistance is endless. Once again, the process of SpiritSinging is about choosing to say *yes* to what you want to create, empowering your vision instead of your fear. Ultimately, it is a choice to reinvent your life, where the sacred is at the center, and things are just things.

In *The Artist's Way*, Julia Cameron discusses forming a creative cluster, or as she calls it, "Drawing a Sacred Circle." She says, "What we are talking about here is the power of breaking isolation. For recovery *from* something Twelve Step groups seem to work especially well. For recovery *to* something, Creative Clusters show remarkable results."

My friend and journalist Susan Chiat shares this about her experience participating in a song circle:

Ever since I was a little girl, I have always loved to sing. I was a closet singer, preferring to sing in the privacy of my own home or in my car where no one could criticize me. Singing was such a love of mine that I hid it from everyone, including myself.

My very first experiences with a SpiritSong circle challenged me right out of this safe and cozy womb. You mean I had to step inside a circle of mostly strangers and sing out loud? Fortunately, in the SpiritSong process you get to keep your eyes closed! This way, I could stay more connected to myself while I sang rather then being distracted by how I imagined my song was being heard by others. And yet, there is really no audience with the SpiritSong process, at least in the traditional sense.

Instead, the circle is involved in a collective birthing process. A circle of midwives welcomes, supports, and honors your song, no matter what it sounds like. Sometimes my song was sweet and gentle, other times a torrent of emotion flew out, releasing pent-up feelings and frustrations. The process of SpiritSong taught me first about expressing myself and secondly about lovingly accepting whatever sound I was making.

Susan reminds us of a simple but important aspect of the SpiritSong technique. When singing in a song circle begin singing with your eyes closed. With your eyes closed it is easier to lose your self-consciousness and to focus on your song. You may experience the group disappearing entirely, only to be brought back around you with warmth and support when you are ready to receive it.

As with individual SpiritSinging, a SpiritSong circle takes place in sacred space. Everything that we have explored about SpiritSinging so far—authentic expression, singing without words, being present, and listening without judgment—is supported and amplified by the use of sacred space.

At the Way of Song Center, we always clean the space before a circle and often create a beautiful centerpiece. You can use fresh cut flowers or candlelight or ritual objects that are meaningful to you. Depending on the orientation of the group, you might invite participants to bring their own special objects to place in the center of the circle or on an altar created for that purpose. Make sure the centerpiece is easily movable so the circle can be cleared when it is time for individuals to SpiritSing.

SpiritSinging is a very intimate activity and it is important that each member of the circle feel very safe. Group safety is created in several ways. One is by creating sacred space together. Sacred space is protected space, free from outside influences. Because it is inviolate space, the concerns of worldly matters that might distract us from connecting to spirit are left outside.

So the question arises, how does one create sacred space? How does one create this protected and highly intentional space?

Intention is the most important element in creating sacred space. Intention is the focusing of your will and life force to create something from a clear vision. If you clearly know that you want to create sacred space—dedicated and set apart for the sole purpose of connecting with self and spirit—and if you align your intention with that purpose, you will be guided to do whatever is necessary in your specific situation to make it work. For example, you might use candlelight instead of lightbulbs to light your sacred space. Most of all, when each member of the group practices nonjudgment and kindness toward one another, a safe environment flourishes.

Sacred space takes us out of ordinary day-to-day life and opens the possibility for magic to happen. Eco-feminist author Starhawk, in *The Spiral Dance*, defines magic as changing one's consciousness at will. In sacred space we can re-create our reality and ourselves. We are transformed when we go between the worlds—the world of the seen and the world of the unseen—and do spiritual energy work. This internal transformation in turn can change the external world. When you are filled with spirit you carry spirit out into the world.

Another important element in creating safety is clarity about one's comfort level with the opposite sex. If there is any question of your feeling safe and free to express yourself in a mixed gender group, create an all-women's or all-men's circle. I participate in a women's song circle that has met for many years. My husband has a men's circle that meets every week, and they too have been together for years. We both draw enormous strength from our sisters and brothers in song. From time to time our circles open, and men and women sing together.

It is wonderful to have a circle where men and women meet together. While a men's or women's circle might feel like a safer space for some, doing SpiritSong can be an extraordinary way for men and women to be together. It allows women to demonstrate their power as well as their vulnerability, and for men to be vulnerable as well as powerful, and all this takes place in a space that is nonjudgmental, loving, and accepting.

Although it might seem that singing in a song circle would create a feeling of inhibition that we did not experience when we sang alone, in practice it is often just the opposite. Once the safety of the group is established, the circle can hold or be a container for powerful emotions we might not have felt safe experiencing alone.

Lyndsey Watson, a certified SpiritSong teacher, shares a powerful experience from her weekly song circle with two other women:

One day I felt in a place of deep despair and was not consciously in touch with any reason for it. I could not figure it out. Physically, I felt tired and stressed. Emotionally, I wanted to die, to have God pluck me off this earth. Spiritually, I was angry that God had put me here in the first place. I felt life was all just too difficult and painful.

My "song sisters" arrived and we began our weekly ritual of medita-

tion, sharing, and song. Over a period of two years, we had been creating a sacred, safe space where we could completely be ourselves without fear of being judged or shunned. It was a place where we could walk through fear of judgment and talk or sing about whatever we needed. We could do this sharing without editing, with total abandon.

When I began my *SpiritSong*, I focused on my breath, in through my nose, out through my mouth, until my body was ready to let out some sound—first a few sighs, then some "ahh" tones. In my state of despair, as sound came through my lips, my eyes began to leak tears. The more air I let in and sound I released the more rapidly the tears fell. The water of my tears joined the air of my breath to move my emotions, causing them to shift. I soon felt hot, a fire burning in my belly. Not only was there despair, but also anger and rage. I was like a volcano erupting. I continued to sing with no words, and the earth beneath my feet supported the movement of my limbs and the pulse of my soul. My song sisters used drum and rattle to accompany the many rhythms of my body. Words began to float into my song—words of pain and resignation leading to cries of anguish and unrelenting grief. The song lasted about twenty minutes.

And all the while, my song sisters listened with focused, quiet presence. They did not move in toward me to take away my pain. They did not stop me out of fear for my sanity. They listened with love and total acceptance and let me go to the depth of my pain. They allowed me to sob until I was finished, even as the judge in me continued its incessant chant, "You should stop, you're going on too long, you should stop now, no one will love you now."

Have you ever allowed yourself to cry until you were done? I mean really done—no more tears left? The power of that alone is immense—no therapist telling me time is up, no well-meaning friends trying to stop me through their fear for my sanity. But when the tears are added to *some air and some song and, most important, encouragement to be authentic—then you find enough power for a real miracle.*

As Lyndsey's story demonstrates, the power and intimacy of practicing SpiritSong with the loving witness of a song circle cannot be overstated. However, let's remember that this group had been meeting together for over two years and knew each other very well. It can take some time to build trust in each other and the process before allowing such an intense experience to be shared. But the rewards are immense. Lyndsey continues:

> *The miracle took a while to unfold. First, an amazing amount of old, fetid energy was released from my body. At the end of the song, I felt drained, yet lighter—much, much lighter. My song sisters sang me a lullaby and rocked me, giving me a feeling of deep safety and nurturing. After they left, I took a nap from which I awoke refreshed and free. My despair had passed through me. I had been released from its prison. I have great gratitude for those two special women who listened so deeply, with all of their being, and, through their genuine love, led me back to loving myself.*

STARTING A SPIRITSONG CIRCLE

Forming a SpiritSong circle can be as simple as sharing your passion with friends and family. If you choose to invite people who haven't been exposed to this book, I suggest they also begin to work their way through its chapters while participating in the song circle.

You can form a song circle with any group of two or more people who gather to SpiritSing and offer each other loving witness. The ideal size for an ongoing circle is four to eight people. When the circle is larger than eight, it may not be possible for everyone to sing in one session. Sometimes there simply isn't enough listening energy to make space for more than eight singers.

In special circumstances it is possible to share in festival-size song circles. At Paul Winter's Living Music Village, a gathering that happens from time to time at Paul's farm in Connecticut, forty people meet to SpiritSing each morning for five days. It is hard to convey the depth and power created during this retreat. I experienced my definitive spiritual awakening during a similar Music Village in 1985 as a result of spending a week in sacred song circle. It was after those five days of SpiritSinging that I entered into a deep silence and was filled with a direct knowing of spirit.

At that time I also received a vision of what happens at death. I was shown an individual ray of light returning to the sun. I understood this vision to mean that we are made of the same substance as a radiant source of life, and that our individual identity merges back into the greater energy when we die.

After that experience I made a commitment to devote myself to teaching this way of song so that others might experience a similar awakening and joy from their song.

LISTENING IN THE CIRCLE

Authentic, open listening gives each participant a profound, undeniable experience of being heard and honored. This principle is used effectively in Twelve Step groups and at Quaker meetings, where only one person talks at a time. When we share in a SpiritSong circle there is no cross talk or direct response to someone's sharing. Everyone listens intently. The sense of being heard and honored that arises in turn encourages (gives courage) and empowers each person to speak or sing more openly. When an individual makes an offering into the circle, it is greeted with a deep, honoring silence, or a ritualized response from the whole circle such as "So be it" or a simple "Ho!" from the Native American tradition. No other comment is needed.

A very important aspect of creating such empowering and focused listening in a group is that each person understand the following: *Listening is a very precious commodity*. It is an extraordinary gift when someone listens in a loving and focused way. It is imperative that we not squander that gift. As part of our intention to create sacred space, each individual takes care not to overtax anyone's listening capacity. Always consider and balance what will be listened to and how much listening time and energy will be required.

HOW THE CIRCLE RECEIVES A SPIRITSONG

What to do after someone has finished singing is an important issue. We do not offer an interpretation of someone's SpiritSong during the circle. Many times a SpiritSong can powerfully move both the singer and the circle receiving the song. Very strong, even cathartic emotions may arise, or the singer may offer the most delicate and sweet song. We accept all emotions in the circle. After a singer finishes we do not evaluate or comment on the song—we hold silence. This offers a sacred space for the singer to come into completion with the song. The energy of the song often continues after the singing stops, and we allow space for that energy. I often say the song keeps singing after the singer comes to silence.

It can be very intrusive to this very sacred personal space to give any direct feedback to the singer. Feedback also can be perceived as criticism or judgment. Leave the singer plenty of space to feel what they feel. Even though you may feel you have something of value to say about another's SpiritSinging, the demon of judgment is so tricky that I always suggest to err on the side of caution lest the singer feel judged by well-meaning but clumsy feedback.

Another great value in holding silence after someone has sung is that it allows them to transcend the "mind" and remain with the experience longer. It is more valuable to let the singer simply be with the experience, without any pressure to respond to others, than to engage the analytical mind. Soon enough, the mind will rush in and begin to "make meaning" out of the experience. I often invite the whole circle to practice "getting out of their minds."

On the other hand, when the group shares such an intimate experience, the need to respond can develop. One way to handle this need is to sing a group song that expresses the collective feeling that the Spirit-Song brought to the circle. This cannot be planned in advance—just allow it to emerge in the moment.

Another way to work with individuals' response to someone who has just sung is to have an agreement that people in the circle will respond when it is their own time to sing, through their own SpiritSong.

Although we usually recommend silence, in the spirit of keeping your circle fluid you may want to invent other responses to the singer that also take into account the boundaries and needs of the singer. One very delightful response we occasionally use at the Way of Song Center is to invent a small song that affirms something positive for the person who has just sung. For example, we might sing, "Now you are home, you have come home." The whole group joins together in singing this affirmation to the person who has just sung.

Sandy Vorce, a Web site administrator for a large health insurance company, shares this story, taken from her journal, about the first time she sang in a song circle:

> *My turn, fear and excitement as I stand and walk to the center of the circle. I gratefully accept the teacher's outstretched hands putting my own atop hers, steadying my growing anxiety. "Sink down," she instructs, and I bend my knees slightly and try to ground myself. I am self-conscious, aware of others in the circle. "Breathe," ah, the breath brings me to myself. A second breath steadier still. "Now let an ahhh tone come out." A soft quivering "ahhh" ventures forth. "Again, and let it go where it will." Another "ahhh," and this time there is movement, curious, and then the sound builds louder, "Is this me?" my last conscious thought before a surge of energy pours through me. I am launched, hands rise in the air. I am no longer aware of others in the room, though I feel that I am safely held.*

In her account, Sandy mentions her hands being held. Sometimes it is helpful to hold the hands of the singer to help them literally feel "held." It is simple enough to ask people if they would like to have their hands held when they sing, and then find a volunteer in the circle to do so. When holding a singer's hands it is helpful to receive them with your palms up and their palms facing down. In this fashion your hands mirror the flow of your intention to receive the song. Be sensitive to signs from the singer that the time has come to release the hands, allowing them to be more alone with their own energy.

Sandy continues:

There is sound pouring forth, yet I am not singing. Primal, tribal, I am sung. A song not known but familiar. I feel so many things at the same time. I am bigger than my body, filling the room. I sense that I am part of an enormous system I can barely comprehend. I have a knowing that the song is of the earth yet there is also an otherworldly component. I am warm and the colors behind my closed eyes are fiery red and orange. I flow with the sound, the song, the immense freedom of motion unbound. I feel vibration within and without. There is a crescendo, a climax, and another direction. I am not in control yet I am completely secure. Time is suspended until suddenly, yet gently, the song winds down and thought returns. There is a tingling down my arms, and my fingers flicker, my eyelids twitch as my eyes open and try to focus. My knees are rubbery. I am very happy! I look around the circle and see the smiles and nods of the women who have held witness. I exclaim, "Wow," which is so inadequate to describe the experience. A huge smile sticks to my face as I walk back to my seat. We do not process, but there is a moment when we breathe and I return to myself. I feel so honored and so grateful for the circle of song.

LEADING A CIRCLE

In Sandy's story she refers to a SpiritSong facilitator, whom she calls the teacher. This leads to the question of whether your circle should have a facilitator or be an unfacilitated gathering of peers. In my experience it can work either way. When beginning a new SpiritSong circle, it is best to have someone in charge of the flow of the energy, at least until the circle has met together for a substantial amount of time. The facilitator can intercede for the good of the group if an individual forgets and overtaxes the listening of the circle or if someone begins giving feedback. This individual can also stand up and support the person Spirit-Singing. The facilitator also should be able to lead group singing confidently. This by no means needs to be someone with a professional voice—just a person who likes to sing. Anyone can take a turn at leading the circle; however, when it comes to leading songs it is helpful for the facilitator to be able to sing on pitch. If a member wants to lead the circle but is not yet able to sing on pitch, another stronger singer can lead the group singing for that circle.

When leading, give instructions that are simple and clear. It is very important that everyone be clear about the process. When explaining a process I find that it is much more effective to state what is going to happen rather than what isn't going to happen. This may seem obvious, but you would be surprised how often we do the opposite. For example, let's say we want to have sharing around the entire circle where each individual speaks from the heart but only very briefly because we know that listening time is precious. We might say, "Now we are going to share our feelings about new beginnings. Please don't speak for a long time because there are many of us who want to share." A better way to express the idea is "Now we are going to share our feelings about new beginnings. Please keep your comments brief because there are many of us who want to share."

After meeting for a year or so, the need for a facilitator may become less important. When a circle is well established it becomes possible for the circle to flow much more organically.

FLOW OF THE CIRCLE

Starting a song circle might sound complicated. You might think, "Okay, I've called everyone here, now what?" I suggest a simple and consistent structure for a song circle: an opening, the central SpiritSong portion, and a formal closing.

The opening, although it may be very short and very simple, is an important moment. If you set the stage well, the entire circle will flow comfortably. If you are unsure and unclear at the outset, the circle can be negatively affected. It can take a lot of work to get a circle back on track if you have not set the context clearly in the opening.

During the opening, make it clear that the group is leaving "ordinary" reality, the day-to-day world, and entering the magical or sacred world. It is important to take some action that symbolizes entering sacred space. This helps all participants to attune their attention and intention together. At the Way of Song Center we have a consistent ritual for this opening time. The facilitator or a member of the circle sings the opening song—either a freely sung SpiritSong or a song carefully selected to invoke the quality that is intended for that particular evening.

For example, I recently led a SpiritSong circle where the intention was to focus on gratitude. So I opened the circle with a song I had written on Thanksgiving Day. I include it here:

THANKSGIVING
(For Hannah's first Thanksgiving)

On this day of thanksgiving
Let a prayer be heard

Let us join our hands together
And say a sacred word
Let us gaze in the eyes
Of the dear ones that we love
And sing a song of praise
To the sky above

As we give thanks for the harvest
Of our family and our friends
For children growing older
For generations without end
And we give thanks for each moment
That we walk upon the earth
And so this day we recognize
The blessing of our birth

On this day of thanksgiving
We remember the gifts past
By the Indian nation
Into our hands so freely cast
And may we find a way together
To walk on common ground
A many-colored people
All moving to the sound

Of giving thanks for the harvest
Of our family and our friends
For children growing older
For generations without end
And we give thanks for each moment

That we walk upon the earth
And so this day we recognize
The blessing of our birth

Another powerful part of opening the circle is the declaration of intention for the focus of the gathering and the acknowledgment that we are entering ritual or sacred space. We call this moment the invocation. It may be done as a formal prayer or in a more casual manner. Here we invoke the experience that we intend to create. Because all the words we say have special power during the time we are together in sacred space, it is especially powerful to state, in a clear manner and with authority, the reality we intend to create in the song circle.

For example, at the opening I often state, "This is a place of non-judgment, a place where each one is honored and celebrated for who they are in the moment." I call this "speaking it into being." Remember, "In the beginning was the word"—language is highly creative. So speak forth the highest vision you have for the circle as if it is so. I have found that this gives the circle the power to make it so.

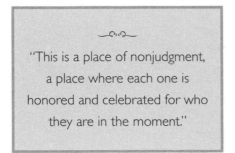

"This is a place of nonjudgment, a place where each one is honored and celebrated for who they are in the moment."

After the opening and invocation, it is time to move into the body of the song circle process. Each member needs to share some energy with the others and to say hello. Each person can briefly report on what is going on in their life, or just say how they feel in the present moment. This is a sort of "how are you" time to check in with one another. The level of intimacy and sharing can vary greatly depending on whether the people are new to each other or a longtime, ongoing circle of friends.

With a brand-new group it is amazingly powerful to have each person share one word to describe how they feel at the moment. Of course, in a SpiritSong circle we often *sing* the one word rather than say it—putting the sound of the feeling into the songword. A general rule is to experiment with singing as many things as possible that we would normally express with speech. It is wonderful to see how much more comfortable a new group will feel after a round of singing "*scared*" and "*nervous*," and then laughing together.

You can also take a few minutes for each person to tell a story about the experience of singing in their lives. For some people singing has been a fearful or shaming experience. For others singing may have been a wonderful refuge. As we learn about one another's experiences with song we can open much more easily to each other with compassion and support when the time comes for individual SpiritSinging.

SINGING TOGETHER

The next part of the process is to sing simple songs and chants together as a group.

Singing together is a joy. We use songs to raise the group energy, to quiet the group energy, and to deepen and express a feeling that is shared in the circle. It builds the community and brings the energy of the group back to a focused place. There is an unmistakable healing that occurs from simply joining our

> There is an unmistakable healing that occurs from simply joining our voices together.

voices together. And then there's harmony. Harmony as defined by Pete Seeger is singing any note that someone else isn't singing at the same time. The pleasure and listening that occur when you add harmony are awesome.

It can be helpful to break up the individual SpiritSinging with group singing breaks. That way, people can release some of the energy they have absorbed by such deep listening. Some groups prefer to remain silent until everyone has finished their SpiritSong. Experiment with singing in between SpiritSongs and let the group decide whether they like the group singing or silence during the SpiritSong time.

Throughout the song circle meeting, we use group singing to make a smooth and elegant transition from one activity to another. For example, when we end our check-in time at the beginning of the circle and before we begin to ground together is a good time for a group song. I have made it a study to pick just the right song—providing the perfect energy—to move from one focus to another. It is really a high art. The power of song cannot be underestimated. When you sing the right song at the right moment, you can feel the energy of the song circle go into a deep union with spirit.

It is helpful to come to the circle with a short list of easy songs and chants that you can choose from. The most important thing is that it be simple and easy to learn. Experiment with using a rousing song after a quiet activity to raise the energy and a gentle song after a more energetic activity to bring the energy to a more quiet and focused place. As you experiment, you will see the undeniable power of a song to move group energy.

SPIRITSINGING IN A SONG CIRCLE

So now we come to the heart of the matter, the individual SpiritSong practice itself. As we know, this means first grounding, using the water breath, and then singing. In a song circle you can join together in a group grounding exercise. This makes a useful transition from the opening into the SpiritSinging. It signals the importance of grounding for each individual who will stand and sing, and it grounds each member of the circle, which prepares them for both singing and receiving songs.

To ground as a group, we do a few simple physical exercises, such as bouncing gently in the knees, rotating the pelvis, and rolling the shoulders. Then we visualize energy pouring from the top of our heads down through our feet and into the earth.

After we have grounded as a group, we usually chant three OMs together to unify us. Then it is time to open the circle for SpiritSinging. At the Way of Song Center, when we say "open the circle" we mean it quite literally. We move the centerpiece out of the circle, clearing it for the singing to begin. This is a physical ritual that we can all see and feel—making space for the song at the heart, the center, of the circle.

What is most important now is intention. It is at this point that all participants focus on the intention of giving time and space to Spirit-Song. A tension usually runs through the group as each person checks internally and asks the question "Is it my time to sing?"

At this point it is important to be aware that there is some courage involved in stepping forward. This is a very different way of interacting than is customary in our culture and it may seem strange or even frightening to some people at first. It can be useful to acknowledge this. I had a student in my early years of teaching this work who called SpiritSong "the fear workshop." Many studies have shown that people's number-one fear is speaking in front of a group. For many, *singing* in front of a group seems totally outside the realm of possibility.

The first person to sing often sets the tone for the rest of the singers. If it is a new circle, and some or all of the people have never been present at a SpiritSong or toning session, it can be helpful to have an experienced singer go first.

I am reminded of the first time I walked on fire. My friend Michael Sky, author of several wonderful books including *Dancing with the Fire*, was the leader that night. It was his job to walk first. If Michael had not been absolutely certain that he could make it across the fire without being burned, the entire firewalk might not have happened. Once I saw him actually walk across the coals, my mind snapped. "This is possible," I thought—whereas "This is impossible" is what I had believed just a few seconds earlier. Seeing is believing. Before my mind could change back to its old pattern of belief, my shoes were off and I had walked across the fire without a burn myself.

I've assisted many people with their first SpiritSong, and after a few minutes of singing, often their eyes pop open in amazement and they say, "I can't believe that voice is me! I've never sung like that before in my life."

I have had the honor of being the midwife to many a voice being born. Daphne Petri, a SpiritSong facilitator, wrote a song about the honor of initiating others into the sacred way of song. It says:

We are the midwives of passion
We are the midwives of song
We come together
To celebrate the birth of our song.

After the first SpiritSong, the circle then opens for anyone who feels moved to sing next. In an established, ongoing song circle, any member can sing first, second, or last as she or he is moved. It is important that each person feel free to choose to sing or not to sing. Putting pressure on people to SpiritSing would be like pressuring them to walk on fire when they weren't ready. For those of us who love to sing, it can be hard to imagine how terrifying this simple act can be for others. Gentle encouragement can be most helpful for someone who wants to sing but is feeling scared.

Once someone gets up the courage to sing, fear usually turns to excitement. "It feels so good to sing!" That's the comment I hear most often when somebody new steps into the center and sings. Our bodies love to sing. Singing brings us increased health. Our minds love to sing because it stops the endless barrage of judging and evaluating. SpiritSinging brings us the freedom to be authentically ourselves, and our souls virtually dance at the chance to express our truth so freely.

As mentioned earlier, SpiritSinging in a group requires a lot of listening. After receiving the songs of the circle, everyone may be feeling very full. This is the time to either do a closing or initiate a group process where everyone can "empty" some of the feelings and vibrations they received during the circle. For example, the whole circle can tone jam—tone together—freely releasing what they are holding.

Finally we complete the circle with the closing section. As with the opening, this is the moment when we pass from sacred space back into ordinary reality. It is important to mark this passage so people feel clear and grounded as they are about to reenter the "real world." The group can sing a closing song followed by a closing prayer or words, and an acknowledgment that "the circle is open but unbroken." We usually join hands during the closing words.

In time, some of the people you have gathered may decide that the song circle is a very important part of their lives. When the group commits to regular ongoing meetings, a true community of song is created.

PRACTICES

1. Continue your daily SpiritSinging and journaling practice as outlined in chapter 2.

2. Secure an appropriate location in which to hold a SpiritSong circle. It should be large and private enough to turn into sacred space for your group.

3. Invite two to seven people to attend the circle. Be sure they have some understanding of the practice and purpose of Spirit-Singing.

4. Make a plan for the flow of your first circle. Consult the sample SpiritSong circles in the appendix, if you wish.

5. Have a wonderful time with your circle.

6. Schedule another meeting with your SpiritSong circle.

7. After the SpiritSong circle, take some time to reflect on your experience. Did it go smoothly? What worked best? Was there anything you'd do differently? Make sure you celebrate that you did it!

9

DOORWAYS TO OTHER DIMENSIONS

Sometimes I sing, most times I am sung.

When I sing, I give sound to emotion, I allow tone to move blockages healing physical ailments, I release stress, I rejoice. When I am sung, I connect with worlds within and without, I become a channel for the earth and for the energies of the universe, I transform beyond form, I connect with the mysteries, I go beyond.

When I sing, I see color
When I am sung, I see light
When I sing, I feel empowered
When I am sung, I feel power

When I sing, I move energy
When I am sung, the energy moves through me
When I sing, I connect with myself
When I am sung, I connect with the Divine

—SANDY VORCE

*O*NE OF THE MOST STARTLING RESULTS OF MY SPIRITSONG TEACH-ing and personal practice has been an unexpected opening to other dimensions. During the nearly twenty years I have practiced SpiritSong, I've experienced a number of multidimensional, or shamanistic, occur-rences.

The first time it happened was about three years into my practice. I was SpiritSinging in a song circle when suddenly my awareness of the circle disappeared. I was, as far as my mind and senses could tell, singing at the sacred site of Mount Sinai. It was as if I had traveled on the song across space and time and been transported to Egypt.

While it was happening, it seemed completely natural. I could feel the desert all around me. I had my arms uplifted to the sacred mount as I sang. When I finished singing, my awareness returned to the circle, but I felt as though I really had just returned from Mount Sinai. At first I was surprised and slightly disoriented. After fully grounding I found my "journey" had been a wonderful experience. I felt blessed by having sung at such an ancient and sacred site and amazed that the song had taken me there.

I can honestly say that even after many years it is not by my will that I travel on song. It is something that the song decides. Occasionally a song decides to take me on a journey, but often it does not. My practice of allowing the song to sing me is the mechanism that enables the song to take me journeying.

The song has also taken me to other dimensions of consciousness. Yogis and shamans have long understood that song is the portal to altered consciousness. Don Campbell, an internationally recognized expert on sound healing, talks about this in his book, *The Mozart Effect*. He says:

The roots of shamanic and indigenous music reach back to the dawn of civilization, when the sound of the drum, rattle, and other primitive instruments would bring communities together, launch the crop plantings and the harvests. . . . The Shaman, an extremely broad term for an ancient healer, invoked great spirits to heal and protect individuals as well as tribes and families. Sounds were the medium through which prayer, invocation, and exorcism took place. It was felt that music and sound magically allowed the powers above and below to come together. The shaman was the bridge between the worlds, able to call down, call up, cast out, and subdue the denizens of heaven and earth.

Like the indigenous shamans, using a drum or a rattle is helpful when journeying with song. Here is another SpiritSinger's story of a journey with song. This one yielded an animal totem or spirit animal helper. Notice that she uses a drum while singing.

I reached for the drum. I journeyed with the drum. I began to see things fairly clearly. I was traveling down, I felt safe and the place felt familiar. I was making sounds as I drummed. I was sitting facing north, the drum up on my right side. I had thought before I started that I would ask spirit animals to appear, but I didn't do this exactly. . . . I just saw myself sitting in this deep safe cave, I saw myself with a blanket wrapped around my shoulders, I was seeing myself from behind. Then suddenly I was inside myself, and I was aware of the presence of a great creature behind me . . . huge and powerful . . . and I felt safe and unthreatened. I felt the spirit of the creature wrap around me, embrace me in its powerful presence, and I was aware that it was a great bear, standing up on its hind legs. There was the shadow of itself behind me. . . . I didn't actually see its face or front . . . I felt its presence behind me, and then I saw it from behind, a huge bear . . . black I think . . . or brown . . .

and I relaxed into its presence. Suddenly I found my hands moving upward on either side of me into an open position of receiving, and I was aware of a deep understanding. This great bear was here to protect me in this deep place I was in . . . and would stand behind me as I walk through my life. A guardian. A powerful strength that would be present when I journeyed deep, when I traveled into dark territory. When I felt fear, the great bear would be there behind and within me.

In his book *Sounds of Healing,* Dr. Mitchell Gaynor, an oncologist at a leading New York hospital, comments on traditional shamanistic practices with song:

The passage from an ordinary state of awareness to a shamanistic state of consciousness is further facilitated by "power songs" chanted by the Shaman. These songs, which mostly consist of a simple melody and a repetitious beat, may affect the central nervous system in much the same way that deep yoga breathing can slow the heart-rate and pulse, as a practitioner moves into a trancelike state.

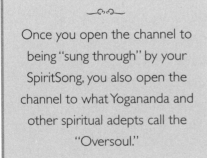

Once you open the channel to being "sung through" by your SpiritSong, you also open the channel to what Yogananda and other spiritual adepts call the "Oversoul."

In my own experience, once you open the channel to being "sung through" by your SpiritSong, you also open the channel to what Yogananda and other spiritual adepts call the "Oversoul." The Oversoul is a body of awareness in another dimension, one that is unseen. I experienced this opening as access to a higher dimension of information. While initially a very startling experience, the opening has been a true gift for me. This enhanced ability to receive guidance has also benefited many of my students and song healing clients.

I am not alone in this experience. Dr. Gaynor also speaks about opening his intuitive channel through working with sound. He observes that "Sound healing practices have helped me to develop my own intuitive sense, and the resulting insights I have had into emotions and feelings have greatly benefited my patients."

Many people are now experiencing an opening to other dimensions. They may call the opening intuition, or channeling, or any number of other terms. Whatever you call it, when it happens it can be unsettling at first. Author Deena Metzger, on her Web site www.deenametzger.com, offers this description of what she calls a "transmission" from a "Transmission Letter" she received in 1986.

This letter could be included in a Doris Lessing novel, in one of the Canopus in Argos: Archives series, Shikasta, for example. But this isn't science fiction. I think it's in the nature of a transmission, embarrassing, frightening, perplexing as this thought is. And I wouldn't dare write this letter, even to my dearest friends, if I were not compelled to do it.

When I heard the voice there was no sound, neither internally nor externally, only the undeniable presence of a voice, as if voice were space or form or image of something beyond these and beyond my understanding. As if voice were silence, and it was exactly in that absolute silence that I recognized its verity.

The voice said, "If there is a chance to save the planet it is only through altering consciousness and behavior so profoundly that a nuclear holocaust will not be inflicted to stop the proliferation of a species which, having lost its humanity as it developed technology, is dangerous not only to itself but to the cosmos. More than the planet is at stake. The work is not to prevent nuclear war, but to establish a vision and initiate reculturalization so that a nuclear holocaust will not be inevitable before life can start up anew."

You can see from this passionate transmission document that such multidimensional encounters can have profound significance for us. It was through working with SpiritSong that I began to receive my own "transmissions." My experience was similar to Deena Metzger's in that I was disconcerted at first and very uncertain about who or what I was receiving. I probably would have ignored the "voices" entirely except that they only came when I was offering a song healing session and were for the specific benefit of the person I was working with.

For example, I worked with a woman who had been suffering with clinical depression. In asking for information to help her I was told to tell her to make art when she was feeling the paralysis of depression. Before the session I had not known that she was an avid craftsperson. Through my interaction with the higher dimensions, I arrived at the helpful suggestion to make art. Now, when things get particularly hard, she makes medicine pouches and her energy picks up.

After many years of receiving these "transmissions," I have determined that they are beneficial for my SpiritSong clients and offer information I could not otherwise access. I have found that now I can easily access this flow of information. To open the channel I simply intend to make contact with the greater consciousness; then I say this prayer: "I open now to the beings of the Way of Song. I ask that only the highest come through for the benefit of all." After this prayer I am connected to a higher vibration and a transmission comes through me.

I thought it would be useful to include in this book some information obtained in this way. I followed the simple process described above and then spoke into a tape recorder. The following is a transcription of what I received.

SpiritSong by its very nature is of other dimensions. There can be no SpiritSong without relationship with other dimensions. This notion you have that the song is personal, meaning particular to you, is erroneous. The song is by its very nature transpersonal, flowing from spiritual force through the wires of your fine bodies and back into the realm of the spirit.

Your very breath is spirit. Consider for a moment that there is no you in a certain sense. For you, who are seeking this information, clearly there is a you; and it is to you that we speak. But also under-

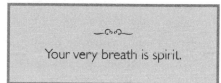

Your very breath is spirit.

stand that within the you, you exist within multidimensional reality. There are aspects of living, aspects of life, that are unseen and unrecognized by you. Breath is one such example. The breath comes in and out of you yet you are not consciously aware of it. You have no control over when the breath within you would stop. This is transcendent to you and yet moves through you in the most individual and particular way. And in the exact same way the song moves through you, exactly as the breath does.

You do not create the arising of the breath, the life force energy of the breath, nor do you create the life force energy of the song, and yet it is completely fluid and natural that it would move through you with force and in fact be colored by the lens of your personality, and in this regard you are very much part of the flow.

You might say your song exists within the song reality, which is a subset of the God reality. It is a bandwidth of the God force. The song reality, or the song dimension, intersects with your reality, your personality, on the body level.

When you are angry or having disturbing thoughts, the song interacts with the disturbing thoughts the way a light might shine through a prism. *Your thoughts become the filter through which the song sings. The great loving flow of song will work consciously—that is to say, will work with the consciousness of the song, not the consciousness of the individual—to flow through that prism and clear it of any impurities, for the song comes from the God force, the Goddess if you will, and returns to the Goddess. In this way, if the song finds any impurities in the channel through which it flows, it will work to dispel these impurities, which we also might call blocks to energy. This is true in the physical and the emotional realms. And so your experience may be very personal, but the song is transpersonal.*

The very nature of the SpiritSong experience is multidimensional, whether you recognize this or subscribe to this model of understanding your experience or not. However, on the other side of this, it is so native, so common and simple and natural for a body to sound that you could say that it is the most embodied and unmultidimensional experience one might have. So to be most accurate one would have to say song is both multidimensional and intimately of this earth body dimension. It is a paradox.

There are only two realities. There is the love reality and the fear reality. You have been trained, you have been chained, you have been restrained behind bars of fear. You are like a circus animal in a cage. Your true power has been completely circumscribed, and that power is the power of love. You have not met this power. You do not know it. You do not even understand the term power, *because for you it is filled with fear.*

But like a lion, through your mighty roar you can begin to have hints of your true power. For actually like the lion that is caged, the strongest resemblance to the true power of your being resides within your voice.

Your voice is your ticket out of the circus cage and into a larger realm, realms that exceed yourself, as you know yourself. Your voice is also your ticket out of the cage of fear. The voice is the passageway allowing you to go through the bars that the body cannot pass through and that the conditioned mind cannot pass through.

Do roar. Do feel this vibration throughout your body. This will move you. By roaring you will travel beyond this limited confinement you know to be your existence.

There are those of you who carry experiences that have been shattering—shattering to the being—and the being has partially fled. This shattering can only be reconstructed by the voice in combination with the community. It not possible for the being to reconstruct this shattered soul alone. This also is true of much of the healing we have spoken of. Healing is a great love that moves through us. The song is an emanation of this love.

Deep healing requires many hands. To heal the planet, which is so ill at this time, it will take many hearts, and songs, and hands: voices joined, hands joined, wills joined, hearts joined in a great web of loving intent—that is to say, fearless intention.

The Song Way can weave a web through many differences in cultures. It can build bridges between many different nodes of this network. Barriers will be much more easily dissolved by the Song Way. It is more powerful than you know.

There is great pain upon the planet at this time. Do not concede to this state of anguish. Do not imagine that you are powerless. You would be amazed if you could view your world from a more distant perspective and contemplate the power of this simple process of song.

Song can dispel profound darkness, heal deep wounding, and cause a greater flow of higher truth, which is to say love. This means that the possibility exists of shifting the frequency from fear to love, through this simple act of song, song with surrender. We are speaking about surrendering to the true nature of song as it moves through your bodies.

To become a greater channel of song, surrendering more deeply to the song, what is required is a shift in one's awareness. One has to commit, make an act of will, to turn one's attention away from daily concerns, away from the endless chatter of the personality/mind, and focus one's attention on the kinesthetic sense of the song. Ultimately, the mind chatter can become silent if one attends carefully enough to the song.

Another way to think about the relationship with the song is as the experience of a passionate love affair. It is an act of union not unlike that with the beloved. It requires a faith that the song is good for us, right for us.

Often you may be frightened that the song will overtake you, pulling you down like a wave or undertow into emotional experiences you do not wish to experience. Due to these fears, resistance arises. So faith is required, that the very nature of the song is like mother love, great love, the sweet love of the mother.

Please understand that mother love could also be understood as father love or any other divine or universal love—choose whichever brings more ease or comfort to you. It will bring ease knowing that the song is the greatest love, come to be with you. If you simply open to this possibility, it will overtake you and you will flow on the field of song. It will carry you many places—some within the emotional realm that you are familiar with, and some to other realms that you might not even be aware of. Work with the song fearlessly and allow it to carry you into new territory. Allow it to show you other possible places and times, both on the planet in this time and in other times.

It is possible to visit your past lives and also other time/space continuums on the current of the song. This is at the discretion of the song. You cannot journey as a pure act of your will, but you can learn how to surf these currents. You can become familiar with the *Way of Song* as a surfer might learn to ride the waves of the ocean.

A FINAL NOTE

The Way of Song is a lifelong journey that offers health, creativity, a doorway into other dimensions, and union with the divine. It is big medicine.

When I asked in song if there was anything else to include here, I found these words: The act of creating is the act of union with the God force. Allow yourself to create freely. Allow the song to sing you freely, and you will experience freedom, true freedom.

APPENDIX:
SAMPLE SPIRITSONG CIRCLES

Use these sample circles as one might use a recipe. Add or take out songs and processes to taste.

SAMPLE 1: THE SPIRITSONG PROCESS FOR A FIRST MEETING

- Prepare the space before the circle meets (see chapter 2).
- Welcome everyone.
- Opening Group Song: "Come Earth and Air."

Opening Invocation

Leader: "We give gratitude for this gathering. We ask that all who have come here find their true voice. We ask that the current of song bless and heal us. We acknowledge our excitement and our fear. Let our fear be washed away in the healing current of song. Let any shame be melted in the warmth of love and acceptance of the circle. May we freely express our truth."

You may want to add, "Now it is spoken. May it only be for the highest good of all. So be it." And have everyone repeat, "So be it."

Opening Name Process

Leader: "Let's find out who is here tonight. We'll go around the circle and each person can say their name, then sing it. The entire circle will sing your name back to you the same way you did it, as a way of welcoming you and letting you know for certain that you have been heard and received. Please keep it simple. If you sing an aria, you'll sound great but it will be too complex for us to remember and sing back to you. And by all means have fun!"

Please keep in mind that this can be one of the most frightening moments faced by a newcomer to the song circle. Remember, it is a brand-new group, and many people feel shame about singing in public. Remind everyone to keep breathing freely and deeply, especially if they are very shy about singing their name. Fear is just excitement without the breath. Breathing deeply gets them over the hump of fear into excitement and into singing. As soon as we hear our name sung back to us, any fear completely melts.

- Group Song: "Flowing Like a River"

One Word Check-In

Leader: "Now let's take a moment to check in and see how we're feeling in this moment. Find one word that best represents how you are feeling. Now let's go around the circle and each of you will sing your one word, exploring how you can create the sound that the word expresses. Begin by saying, 'I am feeling' or 'I am bringing,' and then sing your word."

The leader goes first to give an example of how it is done. Have fun with this. Often there is a lot of laughter as people honestly express how they are feeling and we get to hear the sound of that feeling.

- Group Song: "Michael Row the Boat Ashore"

Introduce SpiritSong Concepts

Leader: "Soon we will begin the SpiritSinging, but before we do, let's consider several things.

"First of all, this is a way of singing where there are no wrong notes. You can't do it wrong, because you're making it up. It's not like singing a composed piece where you either hit the right or the wrong note. Since you are creating the song in the moment, it *cannot be wrong*. The only way anything can be wrong with your song is if you yourself judge it as bad, or not good enough, or anything other than 'it is what it is.' I encourage and invite each of you to check the critic, or the inner judge, at the door.

"We are all well trained in judgment and criticism. This is a culture where almost everything is either overtly or covertly competitive. From our earliest school experience we have been graded and judged. Now we are asking you to change this habit and to enter the 'judgment-free zone.' You will find it is a great relief to suspend judgment, even for a short while. When we SpiritSong, we suspend any judgment of what comes out—we just allow ourselves to sing.

"Another important consideration is that this is not a performance. A SpiritSong is a profound encounter with you, for yourself. Even though there are other people in the circle, they are not an audience. Those witnessing have the rare privilege and honor to be in your presence while you are making this sacred connection with self through the practice of song.

"Finally, have fun. Singing feels great. Our bodies love to sing. Our bodies know how to sing when we just stop judging ourselves long enough to let the natural wisdom of the body take over. Everybody has a voice, so everybody sings. I am reminded of the saying 'If you can walk you can dance, if you can talk you can sing.' "

Group Toning

Leader: "Everyone breathe in through the nose and out through the mouth. Let's do that three or four times. Now the next time you breathe out make a sigh. Then the next time sigh even longer. (Continue to do this until the entire group is sounding a long tone together.) Let's continue to tone together for three or four tones. After the last tone, allow a long silence for each participant to feel the movement of energy that just occurred. This is the beginning of all SpiritSongs: breathe in through the nose, and tone. Now let's stand up and do a grounding exercise."

Grounding: The Tree Meditation

Leader: (Speak slowly, allowing time for each area of focus.) "Begin to feel the energy in your head. Feel it as a thick honeylike substance. Now allow it to flow down into your throat, then into the chest, feel it in your belly, in the pelvis, then the thighs, then in the calves, and finally feel the energy in your feet. Focus on the energy in your feet and really feel your feet in contact with the earth. Now allow the energy to flow through your feet, through the floor, and down into the ground. Feel roots going down to the ground, sinking deep into the earth, down into the core of the earth.

"Now when you breathe in, pull the energy of the earth up into your feet. When you breathe out, feel the energy go deep into the earth. Continue to breathe earth energy in and out, allowing the earth energy to rise higher and higher up the body until it reaches the heart.

"Lift up your arms and feel the heavenly energy of the sky, the sun, and the stars pouring into your hands and arms. Allow this energy to pour into the crown of your head until it reaches the heart and mixes with the earth energy. Stand and breathe and feel the union of these two energies within your heart. Then allow all the energy to flow back into the feet and root deeply in the earth.

"From this place of powerful grounding, let's tone together again. Once again breathe in through your nose and out through your mouth, and allow that breath to move into a tone." The leader begins a tone and the circle follows. Tone three times or until the energy subsides. Allow the silence to remain as each person senses the changes the toning has created within. Then everyone sits in the circle again.

- Group Song: "Swing Low, Sweet Chariot"

Invitation to SpiritSing

Leader: "Now we have come to the heart of the matter, the center of our practice together. It is time for us to allow individuals, when they are moved to do so, to come to the center of the circle and SpiritSing. Together let us create a judgment-free zone. Let us remember that this is not a performance but rather a time to deeply explore our song in this moment. This is a time to allow the song to emerge—to allow us to be sung. It is a time to practice listening to your song without judgment or expectations. For those listening in the circle, remember that it is a great honor to be allowed to witness someone as they sing their song. We too will practice listening without judgment."

The leader sings the first SpiritSong, then directly invites people to sing. At first there may be a long pause as individuals experience feelings of excitement and fear. Allow the pause to occur. Eventually someone will step forward. In the event that no one volunteers, lead another group song and repeat the invitation at the end of the group song, saying, "Who would like to sing?"

- Some suggested group songs: "Deep in the Heart," "Born of Water," "The Earth Is Our Mother"

Continue with time for individual SpiritSinging until everyone who wishes has had an opportunity to sing. It is not necessary that everyone SpiritSings in an evening.

When SpiritSinging is complete, acknowledge all who sang, and formally indicate that SpiritSong time is closed. You might do this by replacing the centerpiece, or any other gesture that you devise.

- Closing Group Song: "I Am Receiving"

Closing Prayer
You may want to join hands around the circle.

Leader: "We give great gratitude for our time together, for the way of song, for the beauty and the courage of the singers. We honor and celebrate each individual voice. We ask that each of us carry the strength and love of this circle into the world, knowing that our voice is unique and valuable and empowered to speak our truth. Now it is spoken. It can only be for good to all. So be it."

SAMPLE 2: SPIRITSONG CIRCLE—GOING WITH THE FLOW

Prepare the space before the circle meets (see chapter 2).

- Opening Song: "Born of Water"

Opening Invocation

Leader: "We give great thanks for this gathering for the Way of Song. We acknowledge that there is a flowing, life-filled song unique to each of us, which can be expressed and received with love. We open now to allow this SpiritSong to flow through us and to listen with compassion and acceptance."

Check-In

Leader: "Let's go around the room and take a few minutes to share what our week has been like, especially what differences, if any, we experienced as a result of our song circle last week. We will pass a talking stick so each person has a chance to speak uninterrupted.

"A talking stick is from the Native American tradition. When the community had a decision to make they would gather in a circle, and anyone who wished to speak could do so while holding the talking stick. When a person has the talking stick they speak for as long as they wish, and everyone else is silent. Any decision required a consensus, which might not be reached until the stick was passed many times. Honoring the stick facilitates the deep listening required to build consensus.

"Let's remember that spirit of deep listening as we each check in about our week." After each person has shared, sing a group song.

- Group Song: "Neesa, Neesa, Neesa" (a round)

Tone Jam

Leader: "Now we're going to do some SpiritSinging together, all at the same time. Under the umbrella of all the sound you can freely explore your voice. With all the singing going on, the challenge is to continue listening to yourself. How very much like life—where we are continually challenged to listen to ourselves in a noisy world. Before we begin this, let's spend some time grounding ourselves. Please stand up."

Grounding

Leader: (Speak slowly, allowing time for each area of focus.) "Begin to feel energy in your head. Feel it as a thick honeylike substance. Now allow it to flow down into your throat, then into the chest, feel it in your belly, in the pelvis, then the thighs, then in the calves, and finally feel the energy in your feet. Focus on the energy in your feet and really feel your feet in contact with the earth. Now allow the energy to flow through your feet, through the floor, and down into the ground. Feel roots going down to the ground, sinking deep into the earth, down into the core of the earth.

"From this place of deep rootedness in the earth, bring your awareness to your breath. Using the water breath, breathe in through your nose and out through your mouth. Now from the bottom of your roots allow a sigh to arise. Breathe again, allowing the sigh to lengthen." The group will sound and then come to silence. Do this several more times.

"Now allow a tone to flow out from the bottom of your feet, and in your own time follow that tone—we will all tone for a long time. Breathe in through the nose, and tone."

NOTE: It is important that a constant sound be maintained so the group feels free to really let go under the cover of sound. If possible allow the sound to die out naturally. Sometimes a few members of a group have energy to continue long after most have stopped. When that occurs, direct everyone to silence and ask that they once again feel their feet.

Leader (after a deep silence): "Now feel your body. Sense any differences—notice how it feels to have sung." Everyone sits.

• Group Song: "Let Your Little Light Shine"

Leader: "Would anyone like to share about what that was like for you?" Allow sharing to unfold.

• Group Song: "Fire Transform Me"

Invitation to SpiritSing

Leader: "Now we're going to open the circle for SpiritSinging. Who would like to sing tonight?"

If no one volunteers, the leader can begin. Sometimes it takes a while before the impulse to sing becomes clear, so it is perfectly all right for the group to sit silently and wait. If no one is ready, you can sing another group song and then ask again.

- Some suggested group songs: "Listen, Listen," "Return Again," "We Circle Around"

When everyone who wants to sing is finished, close the SpiritSinging.

- Group Song: "The Center of the Shield"

Group Meditation

Leader: "Now we are going to do a brief reflection, so make yourself comfortable. Imagine yourself in your own special room. Notice what's in it—all the things that you love and any tools you might need to be creative. Spend some time just looking around your room. Notice a chair placed opposite the doorway. Go and sit in the chair. Make yourself comfortable. Now become aware of the door opening and a beautiful shaft of light pouring through the door. Into the shaft of light steps a teacher. It may be someone you know or an entirely new being. The teacher moves gently through the room to where you are sitting and kneels down beside you.

"Now you become aware of a question. (Pause to give people time to formulate a question.) Ask your teacher the question. Listen for the response. (At this point pause even longer to make sure each person has enough time to really receive an answer.)

"Thank your teacher and watch as she or he slowly rises and walks back out the door. As you sit in your chair in your special room, bring your awareness back to your breath and to this room, and when you are ready, open your eyes." Give the whole group time to make a transition back from trance state to being present in the circle.

"Now we are going to do a pass around the circle where you will have an opportunity to share the teachings you received. If you wish, you can tell us the question and then either speak or sing the answer. If anyone wishes to remain private, simply pass when it is your turn." If possible, have the leader start first as a model, speaking the question and singing the answer. Go around the circle and allow all who wish to share. The guidance each person receives is often quite beautiful and surprising. When the process is completed, the group sings.

- Closing Group Song: "When I'm on My Journey"

Closing

Leader: "We give gratitude for our time together, for all the songs that have been shared and all the deep listening we have offered to one another. We give thanks for the guidance and teachings we have received. Allow the love and acceptance of the circle to be with you. Now it is spoken, it can only be for good to all. So be it."

BIBLIOGRAPHY

Cameron, Julia. *The Artist's Way: A Spiritual Path to Higher Creativity*. New York: Tarcher/Putnam, 1992.

Campbell, Don. *The Mozart Effect: Tapping the Power of Music to Heal the Body, Strengthen the Mind, and Unlock the Creative Spirit*. San Francisco: HarperCollins Publishers, 2001.

Carey, Ken. *Starseed: The Third Millennium: Living in the Posthistoric World*. San Francisco: HarperCollins Publishers, 1991.

Carol, Shawna and Mary Elizabeth Wheeler. *Mystic Soul*. Audio CD. Bedford, MA: SpiritSong Records, 1988.

Chetananda, Swami. *Dynamic Stillness, Part 1: The Practice of Trika Yoga*. Portland, OR: Rudra Press, 1990.

Cope, Stephen. *Yoga and the Quest for the True Self*. New York: Bantam Doubleday Dell, 2000.

Davis, Sheila. *The Craft of Lyric Writing*. Cincinnati: Writers Digest Books, 1989.

Gardner, Kay. *Sounding the Inner Landscape: Music as Medicine*. San Francisco: HarperCollins Publishers, 1997.

Gardner-Gordon, Joy. *Healing Yourself During Pregnancy*. Freedom, CA: The Crossing Press, 1987.

————. *The Healing Voice: Traditional and Contemporary Toning, Chanting and Singing*. Freedom, CA: The Crossing Press, 1993.

Garfield, Leah Maggie. *Sound Medicine: Healing with Music, Voice and Song*. Berkeley, CA: Celestial Arts, 1987.

Gaynor, Mitchell L., M.D. *Sounds of Healing: A Physician Reveals the Therapeutic Power of Sound, Voice and Music*. New York: Broadway Books, 1999.

Hanh, Thich Nhat. *The Miracle of Mindfulness: An Introduction to the Practice of Meditation*. Boston: Beacon Press, 1999.

Jordan, Barbara. *Songwriters Playground: Innovative Exercises in Creative Songwriting*. Los Angeles: Creative Music Marketing, 1993.

Judith, Anodea. *Wheels of Life: A User's Guide to the Chakra System*. St. Paul, MN: Llewellyn Publications, 1987.

Kaufman, Barry Neal. *Happiness Is a Choice*. New York: Fawcett Book Group, 1994.

Keyes, Laurel Elizabeth. *Toning: The Creative Power of the Voice*. Marina del Rey, CA: DeVorss and Company, 1984.

Kumar, Satish. *Path without Destination: An Autobiography*. New York: Eagle Brook/William Morrow, 1978.

Leonard, George. *Mastery: The Keys to Success and Long-Term Fulfillment*. New York: Dutton/Plume, 1992.

Mathieu, W. A. *The Listening Book: Discovering Your Own Music*. Boston: Shambhala Publications, 1991.

Metzger, Deena. *Writing for Your Life: A Guide and Companion to the Inner Worlds*. San Francisco: HarperCollins Publishers, 1992.

————. "Transmission Letter," http://www.deenametzger.com.

Motoyama, Hiroshi. *Theories of the Chakras: Bridge to Higher Consciousness*. Adyar, India: Theophysical Publishing House, 1981.

Sky, Michael. *Breathing: Expanding Your Power and Energy*. Santa Fe: Bear and Co., 1990.

————. *Dancing with the Fire: Transforming Limitation through Firewalking*. Santa Fe: Bear and Co., 1989.

Stam, Kismet Dorothea. *Musings from a Sufi*. New Lebanon, NY: Omega Publications, 1980.

Starhawk. *The Spiral Dance: A Rebirth of the Ancient Religion of the Great Goddess*. San Francisco: HarperCollins Publishers, 1999.

Swimme, Brian. *The Hidden Heart of the Cosmos: Humanity and the New Story*. Maryknoll, NY: Orbis Books, 1999.

Veland, Brenda. *If You Want to Write*. St. Paul: Graywolf Press, 1977.

Weil, Andrew, M.D. *Breathing: The Master Key to Self Healing*. Audio CD. Boulder, Co: Sounds True, 1999.

Yogananda, Paramahansa. *The Autobiography of a Yogi*. Los Angeles: Self Realization Fellowship, 1994.

RESOURCE GUIDE

THE WAY OF SONG AND SPIRITSONG WORKSHOPS AND TRAININGS

For schedule of classes, performances, and workshops, see www.wayofsong.com.

RECORDINGS BY SHAWNA CAROL

Chakra Balancing. Audio CD and chakra cards. Bedford, MA: SpiritSong Records, 2003.

Goddess Chant: Sacred Pleasures. Audio CD. Durham, NC: Ladyslipper, 1998.

The Way of Song: Freeing the Voice Sounding the Spirit. Audio CD. Bedford, MA: SpiritSong Records, 2003.

Above CDs available through www.cdbaby.com, www.barnesandnoble.com, www.amazon.com, and www.wayofsong.com.

Vows: A Songwriter's Sketchbook. Audio CD. Bedford, MA: SpiritSong Records, 2001. Available through the Way of Song Center.

OTHER RECORDINGS

Benedictine Monks of Santo Domingo de Silos. *Chant, Chant II, Soul of Chant*. Audio CD. EMD/Angel.

Das, Krishna. *Pilgrim Heart*. Audio CD. Triloka Records.

Reclaiming. *Chants*. Audio CD. Serpentine.

Roth, Gabrielle. *Ritual*. Audio CD. Raven Recording.

Sophia. *Return*. Audio CD. Hidden Waters Sound.

Ulali. *Mahk Jchi*. Thrush Records.

Various artists. *Women of Wisdom Collection*. Women of Wisdom Foundation.

Most of these are available through Ladyslipper at www.ladyslipper.org.

ADDITIONAL INFORMATION ON THE CHAKRA SYSTEM

Judith, Anodea. *Eastern Body Western Mind: Psychology and the Chakra System as a Path to the Self*. Berkeley, CA: Celestial Arts, 1996. See www.sacredcenters.com for a complete list of Anodea's workshops.

Ozaniec, Naomi. *Chakras: A Beginner's Guide*. London: Hodder & Stoughton, 1999.

Sharamon, Shalila, and Bodo J. Baginski. *The Chakra Handbook*. Wilmot, WI: Lotus Light Publications, 1999.

CHANTING

Gass, Robert, Don Campbell, and Kathleen A. Brehony. *Chanting: Discovering Spirit in Sound*. New York: Bantam Doubleday Dell, 2000.
Kahn, Hayrat Inayat. *The Music of Life*. New Lebanon, NY: Omega Press, 1988.

SOUND HEALING

Beaulieu, John. *Music and Sound in the Healing Arts*. Barrytown, NY: Station Hill Press, 1987.

CREATIVITY

Cameron, Julia. *The Vein of Gold: A Journey to Your Creative Heart*. New York: Tarcher/Putnam, 1996.

OTHER RECOMMENDED BOOKS

Eisler, Riane. *The Chalice and the Blade*. San Francisco: Harper San Francisco, 1988.

Metzger, Deena. *Entering the Ghost River: Meditations on the Theory and Practice of Healing*. Topanga Canyon, CA: Hand to Hand, 2002.